THE REVEAL

AN ANTHOLOGY

TEN AUTHORS COMPILED BY

PUBLISHING, INC.

BEVERLY MORRISON CAESAR

THE REVEAL: AN ANTHOLOGY
Copyright © 2021 by ZizaCreative Publishing

Requests for information should be directed to:
ZizaCreative Publishing, Inc.
718.708.3348
New York

Cover & Interior Design by ZizaCreative Publishing, Inc.
Exterior Photographs by Tina Dawson & Michael Dziedzic

Printed in the United States of America

ISBN: 978-0-578-99868-8

Unless otherwise noted, all scriptures are taken from
The King James Version of The Bible.

- DISCLAIMER -

*Due to the graphic nature of some of the stories, sensitive readers
are encouraged to read with caution and discretion.*

DEDICATION

We dedicate this book to one of the authors,
Mecheall Alston, who succumbed to the Coronavirus in 2020.

Unable to complete his chapter, we honor his sacrifice as he
endeavored to author, "The Tears of a Father."

ACKNOWLEDGEMENTS

The staff of ZizaCreative Publishing wishes to acknowledge the authors and their families for pushing this project through to completion. The journey began in 2018 with a vision to share 12 amazing journeys of God's people with the intended purpose to encourage others.

Life's challenges and vicissitudes came upon us with a pandemic in 2020. Additionally, some families did not want the testimonies of their family members to become public, hence, these brave ten individuals are sharing in this anthology to uplift, encourage and inspire others, in time, to REVEAL their own stories.

This book would not be possible without the faithful dedication of our doctrinal editors, editors in chief, content editors, proofreaders, design and layout editors. Thanks for your untiring press to move forward in excellence.

TABLE OF CONTENTS

Foreword *by Robyn Edwards* 9

Introduction *by Beverly Morrison Caesar* 13

1. A Kept Woman *by Linda Anderson* 25

2. Full Circle *by Ray Ramos* 49

3. Painful Reality *by Donovan & Jennifer Freeman* 69

4. A Glamorous Life *by Lisa Ray* 83

5. Twisted *by David Anderson* 111

6. Little Messenger *by Ana Harris* 119

7. Fight! *by Carly P. Bushelle* 133

8. Heaven for 17 Days *by Shanay Howard* 159

9. Who Am I? *by Pauline Hunter* 173

10. The Other Man *by Elaina Monrae* 181

The Authors 223

FOREWORD

Robyn Edwards

*"I have told you these things so that in Me you may have peace.
In the world you will have tribulation. But take courage;
I have overcome the world!" John 16:33 NIV*

You hold in your hands a powerful collection of testimonies from those who in the body of Christ are more than conquerors in God's kingdom. These God-glorifying testimonies are sensitive and sometimes sacred in nature, but they are crucial for your own encouragement, healing and deliverance. Having experienced my own victories, I join with these brave souls in sharing their glorious testimonies.

Not only are these stories profound, but also they will be an encouragement to those who are found reading this book. Their stories range from parents who have lost children to gunfire, rare diseases, heart attacks and other disappointments. Some are families who have overcome giving birth to children with challenges, others with near death illnesses and many who have conquered the sting of verbal, emotional, physical - and yes, sexual abuse.

My life, being filled with physical, emotional and sexual abuse, could have had a different outcome. However the victories that I have experienced only prove that God is very much alive and ready to give you your own testimony!

If you are holding anger and resentment from your past or present adversities, bitterness will set in and cripple you emotionally for the rest of your days (2 Sam 13:20b). Our bodies were not created to hold anxiety, anger, resentment and hostility.

Jesus tells us in John 16:33 *"in this world you will suffer tribulation;"* that word tribulation can also be translated as pressure, affliction, anguish, burdens, persecution or trouble of some sort. The Pulpit Commentary, written by Donald Spence Jones, explains that Peace is the balance of a calm state of mind; We all need our Lord behind us and His Spirit within us to encounter the tremendous odds displayed against us, in secrecies of life, temptation of the devil, infirmity of the flesh, and antagonism of the world, so that we need not be surprised that He (the Lord Jesus) would tell us to "be of good courage."

Victory has already been achieved over the world's temptations, and over the bitterness of internal torment and treachery, and all human ingratitude; hence the use of the perfect tense, "I have overcome." Just as Jesus overcame the world so many years ago we will be continuous overcomers and conquerors as well.

May the words stated in the famous hymn by the late Stuart Hamblin, "It is no Secret" minister to you:

> *There is no night for in his light you'll never walk alone*
> *You'll always feel at home, wherever you may roam*
> *There is no power that can conquer you while God is on your side*
> *Take him at his promise, don't run away and hide*
>
> *It is no secret what God can do*
> *What he's done for others he'll do for you*
> *With arms wide open he'll pardon you*
> *It is no secret what God can do*

I encourage you to read this book of anthologies and encourage others to do so as well. For in these pages you can find peace and fulfillment as you celebrate with God's people His great victories!

INTRODUCTION

Beverly Morrison Caesar

As Christians, many of us have come to realize that we are not exempt from trouble. We are not exempt from challenges or the vicissitudes of life that come from the east, the west, the north, and the south. For those of us who have life experiences under our belts, we have learned, through the Word of God, that "weeping may endure for a night, but joy comes in the morning."

I was born and raised in the West Indies (WI) and was influenced not only through a strong matriarchal society, but also through the examples of the women in my life. My mom and both of my grandmothers were dominant, strong leaders. When my mom migrated to the United States, she left me and my two sisters to live in "the country" - the rural area - in the care of her mother, whom we affectionately called, "Mammy". In no way was it considered a derogatory expression. As a matter of fact, it wasn't until I migrated to the

US that my reference to my grandmother was questioned as a negative term. Nonetheless, Mammy had the task of ensuring that her daughter's girls were cared for - carefully and cautiously. Dennis, our older brother, was independent enough to manage on his own and so he stayed in the city with our dad.

My grandmother taught us how to cook, wash clothes, clean the house and fulfill all duties related to good housekeeping. Sunday School, Bible study, and church attendance were all part of our discipline. There was one area that was not touched or taught to us at all - relationships with the opposite sex: BOYS. Here are some of the words she told us:

> *"Stay away from boys!"*
> *"If you see a boy walking toward you on the same side of the street, cross over to the other side."*
> *"Don't bring any babies into this house!"*
> *"If a boy tries to talk to you, turn your back and walk away."*

I never had any healthy talks or conversations from either my mom or grandmothers about my personal development as a young girl. No one shared with me the "facts of life." The word sex was taboo and never mentioned. I accidentally learned the harsh realities of being female and the natural occurrences that would unfold in my body as a young developing girl. On the other hand, my older sister and her friends were usually huddled together talking about "secrets" that they said I was too young to learn about. I was shunned from their conversations and was left to fend for myself. Bottom line, I grew up naive, shy, uncertain about the "facts of life," and I was what some people call "sheltered." I needed an escape and so I lost myself in books such as Nancy Drew, The Bobbsey Twins and The Hardy Boys. Whenever you saw me, my head was stuck in one of those books.

Back to my sister and her friends: One hot summer day during school recess, I remember seeing them with a booklet that taught about a woman's body and how the menstrual cycle worked. It also taught about the processes of becoming pregnant and childbirth. Here they were again huddled over this booklet, but when I started to ask questions, I was told I was too young. However, one of my bold friends was able to commandeer a copy and we, in turn, huddled over the booklet. To me it was like reading another language. I was totally lost. Nothing made sense since those words were never spoken to me or read in my hearing. I pretended that I understood, but I left feeling lost and confused. I thought that holding hands and kissing a boy would lead to pregnancy! The thought never entered my mind to ask my grandmother about what I saw and glimpsed in that booklet. Her response would have been something like this, "You had no business reading that stuff anyway!"

In 1969, my dad, me and my two sisters migrated to "the

land of the free and the home of the brave" - the good old United States of America. My brother remained in the West Indies to man the house and complete his education. Additionally, he was in a serious relationship, which one year after our migrating to the US, brought us back to the WI to participate in his wedding.

Many people would think that by 17 years of age, I would have grown out of my naïveté. Well, that was not my story. Coming to America pushed me even further into a shell full of inhibition, reclusivity and isolation. I wanted to go back home. America wasn't for me. I did not fit in. My older sister and I shared similar feelings about America, while my younger sister seemed to be adapting quite well. What pulled me out from that place of "shyness" was an active Sunday school at the church we began to attend. The teaching was sound, and the teachers were engaging and created an atmosphere of inclusivity. The youth department was also vivacious, lively, fostered engagement and camaraderie. I slowly began to emerge, to blossom, to make friends, and to be comfortable with who I was becoming as a young adult. Young men began pursuing me, but I shunned them because I was uncomfortable around them, until I met this one young man who tenderly grabbed my interest. Remember, I did not have any experience. I never held hands before and was never kissed by a man before. As a matter of fact, my first kiss wasn't until I was 19, and I was grossed out by it. Imagine that!

After graduating High School, I headed to Hunter College to pursue a degree in Home Economics (HE) with a concentration in clothing and textiles. I remember having to write a term paper for one of my HE classes that dealt with families and children. We had to research and write about the Pros and Cons of Abortion. Research and term papers were my strong suit, so I delved in full force. What I found in my 1975 research was that life did not begin at conception, but at birth. I read and documented the facts that, in pregnancy, in the first trimester what you were carrying was just a glob of flesh – not a child at all, and that it wasn't until the second trimester, that formation was beginning to take shape. I visited the Planned Parenthood organization, interviewed the directors, and left with notes validating their premise that life began at birth. Hence, abortion was not taking a life, plus the decision rested with the mother to be. On the other hand, I interviewed priests who contradicted the Planned Parenthood premise. My paper was so well done that the grade I received was A++. For some reason, I held on to that paper to this day.

Anyway, fashion became a serious interest of mine and so the Fashion Institute of Technology (FIT) was a school that enhanced my interests. It was during this time that I began dating unsaved men. Not ever wanting to be in a serious relationship with any of them, but simply enjoying their company and the dating experience. Yes, I was active in church, singing in the choir, participating in the youth ministry and Sunday school. I saw to it that these young men would come to church with me, and I even went as far as inviting them to meet my family. I knew they would not be in my future permanently, but I enjoyed their company.

One day at age 22, I met an older man, let's call him Joe, who was in his thirties, and that encounter changed my life forever. He had a car, drove for UPS, was a big spender and doted on me. My other dates were in my age range and the public transportation service was our mode of traversing the boroughs, which I never despised. Often Joe would take me and my sisters for a drive around the city. We all liked him.

I was still naive, unwise, foolish, and somewhat childish. Living a sheltered life has its pros and cons. Some parents and guardians try to protect their children from the bombardment of evil that surrounds us every day, by keeping them indoors or under lock and key. They try to protect their children from the realities of an unsafe world by keeping a close watch with tight reins. Then the flip side to this scenario is parents who believe that their children should be exposed to the realities of life at a young age. Go out and explore, see the world, sow some oats, and come back enlightened. Ephesians 6:1 tells us that we should train our children in the way they should go so that when they are old, they will not depart from that training. A reasonable balance is the key along with godly biblical training. Once the child gets to a certain age, the responsibility of their actions rests solely on their shoulders.

Speaking of responsibilities, a decision I made one infamous night in the back seat of Joe's car was solely mine. The truth be told, it was not a pleasant or enjoyable experience at all. I could never tell you what happened, all I remember was that I wanted to get home. One month later, having missed my cycle, the "P" word was now a part of my vocabulary. We kept this information to ourselves. We told no-one, and since I was "knowledgeable" about abortions that was the logical course of action to take. Joe handled everything with the hospital and this "glob of flesh" was expunged from my body. The relief was liberating. The burden was lifted. I was free. Who was I fooling? The guilt was burdensome. Although no one knew, I felt ashamed and embarrassed. I disappointed myself, my family, my church, and my God. Deep down inside, I had this gut feeling that what I did was wrong, even though I genuinely believed, at the time, it was just a "glob of flesh." Although I was not filled with the Holy Spirit, He prodded me so that I became uncomfortable in His presence; I cried, I repented, I begged His forgiveness,

I wanted peace, but it never came because of the unforgive-
ness I struggled with. I could not forgive Joe. How could he
do this to me? He should have known better, he was older
and wiser. Well, he wasn't saved. I had no business being
with him at all. God showed me myself and I did not like
what I saw. I started hating myself. I began losing weight
and I lost my drive.

While I was locked into this painful and private world, my
older sister was dating a young man who lived in Chicago.
She made plans to visit him and his family, and she invited
me to travel with her. That experience was a turning point
in my life - a "Kairos" moment which is a specific moment
in time where God shows up and manifests Himself in such
a way that the moment is forever etched in the mind. To get
right to the point, it was in Chicago, under a summer tent,
with sawdust on the ground where I experienced the bap-
tism in the Holy Spirit. This infilling was new to me, in that
I was not taught about this experience in my former church.
You see, because God was already in my future, and He
knew that I would meet a man of the Pentecostal faith, he
was preparing me for that part of my future life. Although
I had this Kairos moment occurrence, I still struggled with
the overwhelming guilt of my abortion. The disappointing
faces of my church elders, my family and my friends loomed
before me. What would they think, if they knew? Sadness
overwhelmed me left and right causing depression to weigh

on my shoulders. Sleepless nights were my constant companion. Sometimes I wished I would not open my eyes at the dawn of day.

FAST FORWARD TO 1979: I married the love of my life, a pastor, and was functioning in my role as a wife, a mother, and a leader in the church. Women's conferences were a yearly occurrence at the church and nine years into my marriage and two children later, I had another Kairos moment at the conference. It was a Friday night and the speaker encouraged people to be filled with the Spirit or to be refilled. The service was electrifying, and the power of God was evident in the sanctuary. Each of us were having our own private time with the Lord. I myself was lost in His presence in my own corner – basking in His glory. He refilled me and, in that moment, I released all my guilt on Him. The burden had become so heavy that peace evaded me. The guilt haunted me day and night. I was in my own private hell. I couldn't talk to anyone, they wouldn't understand. That night I realized that God had forgiven me the *first* time I asked for His forgiveness just like he heard Daniel's prayer the *first* time he prayed. His answer was held up by an evil spirit, but the angel finally broke through with his answer and told him that God heard his prayer from the first time he prayed. God encouraged me that night. He told me that I had been forgiven; it was now time for me to forgive Joe and to forgive myself. Well, that breakthrough came, and I bolted from my corner and ran around the church praising God. I did not care who was watching or staring. Some people ran with me, others praised from their seats and it's as if the entire church ruptured into extraordinary praise. No one knew why I was running, but the praise was infectious!

Never judge a person because of their "praise break". We don't know what people may be dealing with and how God may be blessing them. Don't allow the sins or mistakes of your past to keep you in bondage. God rewards faithfulness, and He rewarded me above and beyond my expectations. He knew the plans He had for me according to Jer. 29:11, and he saw the genuineness of my heart and rewarded me with a husband, four children and ministries.

I am walking in such freedom from this mistake I made as a 22-year-old naive West Indian girl. Today I can share this testimony without guilt or condemnation. When I finally shared my experience with my entire family, all I received was love and encouragement. Therefore, I can speak with a clear heart and a clean conscience.

May the God who loved you and gave His only Son, Jesus Christ, as a sacrifice for your sins, grant you victory over sin and mistakes. May you walk in the boldness of His Word which is liberating. This book – THE REVEAL – will do just that. It will reveal to you the unconditional love of God in the lives of His people. It is the prayer of this publishing company that this anthology, and these personal testimonies will encourage you to walk in your victories as you over-come by the words of your testimony.

1
A KEPT WOMAN

Linda Anderson

"For I know the plans I have for you," declares the Lord. Plans to prosper and not to harm you. Plans to give you a hope and a future."

It seemed like just another hot, humid August day in Brooklyn, New York. But there was something different about this day. At least it would be for a 42 year-old mother of three boys ages 14, 13, and 10. No one knew when they woke up that morning that this was the day lives would be changed. I imagine that when she woke up that morning and had her usual cup of tea and thought about her day and getting her boys ready for their routine, that the last place this woman thought she would be by the evening, was Kings County Hospital. But on this particular day, August 6, 1962, that is exactly where this middle-aged mother would find herself.

Did one of the boys get hurt? Not inconceivable considering

their ages and they were, after all, boys. Did something happen to her husband or another family member? No, this would be the day that this mother would give birth, for the fourth and last time. This birth would be different. This time she would give birth to a baby girl! Can you imagine being 42 years old, having two teenage boys and one pre-teen boy and being pregnant? I know when I was 42 years old the last thing I wanted to think about was having another child. But here this woman was, after only finding out she was pregnant four or five months earlier giving birth to a baby girl and starting all over again.

Why 10 years after the birth of her youngest child did this woman conceive another child at this time in her life? Who knew what would be in store for this child? What would be her purpose? No one knew, but God had a plan!

I have heard many times from different people "You should write a book". I would laugh, but in my mind, I thought: Me? Why? I am just a girl born and raised in Brooklyn. My parents were not well known or rich and famous people. We were actually quite poor. I had not accomplished anything in my opinion that that other should take note of. There was not anything in my life at that point that I felt was book worthy. I felt no one could be interested in my life. I mean yes, I have had my share of struggles. Many obstacles that I've had to overcome. Been delivered through many a storm. But there are plenty of other women who have gone through what I have experienced and worse. So why should I write about it? And what part of my experience should I write about?

Most of my experiences are not unique to me. Again, there are plenty of other women who have experienced or are experiencing these same things and more devastating. However, I can say that through it ALL God has kept me. There were times when He shielded me. There were times when He hid me in plain sight. And every step of the way He has preserved me!

"For I know the plans I have for you declares the Lord. Plans to prosper and not to harm you. Plans to give you a hope and a future."

I can't think of an area in my life that this scripture hasn't helped me through. When things are going great (in my opinion) I'm reminded that God does have a plan for me. Wonderful things that I never could have imagined. When it feels like my world is crumbling all around me and I feel as though I have no one to turn to, I find comfort in knowing that God does have a plan for me. When I don't know which way to turn or I'm not sure of His plan; I remind myself that He has a purpose for my life; that I'm not a mistake or an accident.

As far back as I can remember I have always had this feeling of being less than. That I wasn't quite good enough. That I wasn't smart enough. That I wasn't accepted by others. I can remember feeling like I did not fit in as if I didn't belong. Yes, I've had and do have friends but never really feeling a sense of belonging. My father died 10 days after my fifth birthday, my mother, who was unable to work for health reasons, did not have a lot of money while I was growing up. As a result, I did not have the latest fashions or the "cool" clothes. I was constantly made fun of. Being light skin with green eyes and having Delgado for a last name certainly didn't help. You see during the 1960's it was not cool, cute or popular to be light-skinned. At least not in Brooklyn where I grew up. I was called "whitey," "high-yellow," etc. People thought I was either white or Hispanic. Not that there is anything wrong with either, but it just wasn't who I was. But no one believed me when I told them I wasn't. And as a child I didn't know how to explain that I was Cape Verdean. You could barely find Cape Verde on the map. No one ever heard of it. I was constantly picked on, ridiculed, beat up and talked about.

Although I was a very bright child and placed in accelerated classes I didn't reach my maximum potential. After leaving elementary school the administration wanted me to skip a grade. However, because of my low self-esteem and feelings of inferiority I listened to the voices that kept telling me I wasn't good enough, not smart enough and wouldn't be successful in life. Listening to those voices caused me to procrastinate and not put my "best foot forward." I felt as if I could never amount to anything *good*. But God DID have a plan for me.

Being called a "Kept Woman" is not good thing (according to the world's standards). Wikipedia describes a kept woman as **"Historically the term has denoted a 'kept woman,' who was maintained in a comfortable (or even lavish) lifestyle by a wealthy man so that she would be available for his sexual pleasure. Such a woman could move between the roles of a mistress and a courtesan depending on her situation and environment."** Looking back over my life, I have come to realize that I was a "Kept Woman" not according to the world's view but according to God's standards and provisions. I was kept in my right mind (even though sometimes my mind was under attack); kept financially, kept emotionally, kept spiritually. I can look back and understand that like Moses was hidden in plain sight when he was in the ark floating down the Nile River as an infant and as a son in Pharaoh's house, God kept me hidden until the appointed time. That's why I never felt like I fit in; I wasn't supposed to fit in! Oh yes, I've made some bad decisions, poor choices and some big mistakes but even in that I was a "Kept Woman." Glory be to God!

Whenever God is up to something in my life, I get an over-whelming feeling of restlessness. Perhaps you have had or are experiencing this same restlessness. I had a sense that I was supposed to do something but was not sure what it was. I would have these feelings of being unsatisfied with my current state or position or circumstance but uncertain of the direction to take. It is not always a comfortable feeling either and I have come to learn that looking to people to give you the answer or some epiphany is not the way to go about settling that restlessness. I can say that from experience. Too often I would look to people to give me the answer, to point me in the direction that I should have taken and to offer some sage advice. But seeking out different people I can tell you that most of the time I was left disappointed and/or confused. I was disappointed because I didn't feel as if I received what I went looking for. I was confused because what I was hearing from them didn't make sense; they didn't really understand my heart or they contradicted the direction that God was trying to take me. No, you must seek God and listen for that still small voice and get peace from knowing you have heard Him. When people speak to you it should only confirm what God has put in your spirit. It should be to shine the light on your understanding of what God is saying and doing in your life. Their words should give clarity to your understanding of what God is saying. We should not seek people to define our purpose but seek "the people" who will guide us in our purpose. People can be very convincing about what you should and should not do – however, it's not always in the way that God is directing you. Don't get me wrong, there have been a few people (and I do mean a few) who listened to me and heard my heart and the voice of God as it pertained to me. These people have spoken over and into my life in ways I can't even begin to explain in this one chapter. Some of these people I sought out and some sought me out. I can honestly say, most of the time when I went seeking in desperation, it was usually to the wrong people. But when God guided my footsteps and provided the opportunity, He had someone for me who would speak life to me.

I can remember one particular time in 2005 that I had that feeling of restlessness. I felt I should be doing more with my life, but what? I felt an urge to go to school, I actually liked school, but I wasn't sure what I should major in. I had a degree in Business Administration so of course the natural thought process was continuing that path. So, I enrolled in Empire State College's Distant Learning Program which was offered through my job. At that time distant learning or online learning was a fairly new concept and not widely accepted. However, I reasoned that I could work at my own pace since I had a job and young children not to mention my church responsibilities to consider. About the same time my church had started a Bible College and I felt drawn to take classes. I did both schools for about one year. At the end of the year, I knew something had to go; the load was too overwhelming. But which one? Empire State College made more sense when considering a career path, but I felt a strong urge to attend Bible College.

Back then I was a single parent, with a daughter in college and three children at home. Since my job was paying for Empire State College in full and up front that seemed like the logical choice. But again, the urge to go to Bible College was so strong that I could not ignore it. At the time, a close friend and someone that I highly respected and whose opinion mattered was counseling me financially to help me get and stay on track. When I mentioned going to Bible College her first response was, "How are you going to use that in a career?" I had no answer. Her next question was, "How are you going to pay for it, it's not in the budget." Again, I had no answer. There really was no money in the budget. Every penny was carefully accounted for. But I knew I had to go. After about a week the conversation came up again. This time my response was a little more adamant. I told her that I did not know how God was going to use this education, but I knew that He was leading me to go and that He would have to work out the payments. With that she replied, "Well if you are not going to listen to me (her financial counsel) then I'm done" and with that she left my house, and we did not speak to each other for several years and to this day our relationship has never been the same. I was very hurt and disappointed for two reasons: firstly, she was someone whose relationship I valued and someone that I looked up to and secondly, as a woman of God I would have expected her to understand and say, "Well let's see how God is going to do this." I didn't know how I was going to pay for school, but I knew I had to go.

I enrolled in Bible College and was very determined. You see that voice was still there telling me I wasn't smart enough. That I was only trying to prove myself to other people in the church. But I was determined to be the best student I could be. God gave me a vision of graduating and not only graduating but at the top of my class! I held on to that vision. I spoke that vision. I saw myself graduating and giving the valedictorian speech at the graduation. I wasn't just concerned with myself but with my classmates as well. There was never any sense of competition but instead we made a pact to help each other get through! Lo and behold in May of 2009 I graduated with a Bachelor's degree and at the top of my class giving the valedictorian speech! Two years later in May 2011, I graduated with my Master's degree – again, valedictorian! Isn't God awesome?! It wasn't so much that I came up with this idea and God made it happen. God had given me the vision of being valedictorian. The Word instructs us to *Delight yourself also in the Lord, and He shall give you the desires of your heart* (Psalm 37:4). I believe that means that God will not only give us what we want, but He will give us the things *to want*. We often just quote and consider verse four, but that verse is sandwiched between verses 3 and 5. The entire passage reads: *"**Trust** in the Lord, and do good; **Dwell** in the land, and **feed** on His faithfulness. **Delight** yourself also in the Lord, And **He shall give** you the desires of your heart. **Commit your way** to the Lord, **Trust** also in Him, And **He shall bring it to pass.**"* (emphasis mine). I trusted the Lord to make away for the tuition to be paid. I dwelt with Him (chose to study the Word, rather than opt for the logical choice of study) and fed on His promises and His faithfulness. I delighted in Him, found peace knowing He would provide, and in turn He gave me the desire to honor Him by being the best student I could be – not better than my classmates, but the best student I could be. As a result, He brought it to pass.

Little did I know back in 2005 that God was preparing me to serve in ministry. But God had a plan and a purpose for my life and I'm grateful. God did not stop there. He gave me the determination to go all the way! After a taking break from school for a few years as I got accustomed to the new shoes that I was wearing, the desire to finish school returned. This time at a different Bible College. In 2014 I enrolled into Bible College with the hopes of getting my Doctorate. After meeting with the Dean, I discovered that I would have to go through their Master's program before I could go on to the Doctorate. I didn't think I had it in me. I already had my Master's and just wanted to get my Doctorate. I did not want to go backwards. But I felt that if I did not go through with it that I would be leaving something undone or incomplete. I thank God for my husband's support and understanding children who encouraged me and sacrificed so I could do what I believe God was leading me to do. So off to school I went. IT WAS HARD! But by the grace of God, I completed the Master's class and went on to receive my Doctorate in May 2016. I can hardly believe that was five years ago. Take that devil! So much for not being smart or good enough! God gave me the ability and kept me through that.

Now talk about giving you the desires of your heart: from the time my children were young, I wanted to have my own childcare business. I was working for the phone company at that time had a great salary and excellent benefits and there was no way I could afford to leave my job. In 1994 a friend had started a childcare business and had asked if I wanted to partner with her. I refused the offer for several reasons. One, it didn't feel like the right thing for me to do, second, I was afraid to give up my salary and benefits and third, I did not have the support of my husband and the time. Bottom line – I was afraid.

So, I continued to work at the phone company for about 18 years. I did love my job. I liked the fact that I had an opportunity to help people. I was proud to work for such a prominent and strong company. During my time there I saw many changes. When I first started it was New York Telephone, then it became NYNEX, next Bell Atlantic and then to what is finally known today as, Verizon. Whew! I always felt it was a great company, but the focus of the company shifted and the job that I was hired for was no longer the same in my opinion.

One day as I was leaving work, I found myself crying in the elevator from the stress of the job. I knew that I had to go. By this time, I was a single parent with four children. I felt like I couldn't leave. How would I support my children? I was afraid. Then opportunity presented itself. Verizon was offering a package to employees as an incentive to leave the company. And it was tempting. Do I take the package or not? What will I do if I did take the package, I would still need to work? The thought of doing childcare began to well up inside of me again but I was still afraid of not earning enough money.

I sought counsel with someone I respected for advice. As it turned out they were about to start a not-for-profit organization and upon hearing my desire to leave the phone company offered me a position as an administrator. With the salary they were offering me and the money that I would receive from my package I would be able to "afford" to leave the phone company. So, I put in my papers and retired! It felt like such a weight being lifted from my shoulders! I was excited for a new beginning. I would work at this not-for-profit corporation and put things in place to start the childcare business. I left the phone company in June and the plan was to start my new position in September. I planned and budgeted my money so that I could take the summer off and spend time with my children doing things I could not do before. It was a great summer.

Then at the end of August I was blindsided. I was informed that the position that was offered to me had to be rescinded regrettably! Panic set in big time. I did not know what I was going to do. I had another month left before I would need that income. I had to find a job! Childcare would have to go on the back burner. Again!

That was 2007. I did find another job, it was $20/hour less that I was making at Verizon, but it was a job. And God still kept me. The bills were paid. We had food to eat. I was grateful. It was also during that time that I became engaged to David W. Anderson. Boy oh boy was my life about to change. I NEVER imagined being married to a man who was a Pastor of a church. Talk about new shoes to walk in! I NEVER saw that coming! Childcare was not only removed from the back burner – it was taken off the stove completely! My focus was now on being a good wife to this man, learning how to walk in the new shoes I found myself wearing and getting adjusted to leaving my church. That last part was so hard for me. Childcare was now the furthest thing on my mind at this point.

Fast forward to 2014. Still working in Workforce Development but for a different organization, I found the desire to do childcare welling up inside of me again. Mind you, it wasn't the first time. There were several occasions that I requested the licensing application and it just sat on the shelf and expired. I never went any further in the process. Again, giving into my fears.

Sometime in the beginning of 2014 I requested another package. And it did sit – until April 25, 2014. On that day I *"just happened"* to have a conversation with a colleague, Donna, who also had a childcare business on the side. When I told her about my desire to do childcare and that I had an application and that it was going to expire on June 1st. She responded, "Oh, so you're a procrastinator! Okay, so here's what we're going to do – you are going to work on your application for 20 minutes everyday until it is complete. I'm going to check on you everyday to make sure you did your 20 minutes. And if you get stuck on anything, I'll help you with it." And that she did. She either called or texted me to make sure I was working on that application. The application process was overwhelming, but God used this friend to nudge me along and get it done.

God is a Master Strategist. I *just happened* to be working in Workforce Development at the time and part of my responsibility was to assist my clients with finding employment. That didn't just mean helping to write and prepare resumes and conducting mock interviews to help them prepare for the real thing, all of which I did. A huge part of my responsibility was to find employers who were looking for candidates and matching them with my clients. Sounds easy right? Wrong! But it did afford me the opportunity to meet a lot of people and make a lot of connections. I had many employers from retail to Temp Agencies, to law offices, restaurants, doctors' offices so many different companies. Oddly enough most of my employers were... you guessed it – childcare providers! I had successfully placed a couple of clients with some providers and the word spread. They were so eager to speak to me about helping them find the right fit for their company. (I didn't understand the reason they were so eager at that time, but I do now!)

In my quest to find more childcare providers, I *happened upon* Little Sponges Childcare and its owner, Linda Castro. I had seen a lot of childcare businesses but when I walked into that center I was blown away. I marveled at the size, the quality of program, the layout and décor and the standard of excellence in that place. Granted no job, company or organization is perfect but I remember thinking, this is how I would want to operate my business. During our many meetings I would listen intently and asked a lot of questions. On the outside it would appear to someone observing that I was doing my due diligence in trying to find the right client to fill her positions but in the back of my mind I was gathering information that I would someday need.

Linda Castro provided a wealth of knowledge and had a genuine heart to share. I found that to be very refreshing. Years earlier when I was considering opening my own childcare business, I tried to meet with various providers to "pick their brain" and get advice and I was amazed at how many people were reluctant to share any information. But that was not the case with Linda Castro! One day I *casually* mentioned that I had requested and received the application to get my childcare license, but I hadn't done much with it and it would be expiring soon.

Immediately she started giving me advice. She called her secretary and had her make my appointment to be finger-printed using her number and scheduled a time for me to return so that she could review what I had completed in the application. I left her office so encouraged, motivated, and excited. I knew that God had ordered my steps and lead me to this woman. Between Linda and Donna guiding me through the paper application part of the licensing process, I was able to complete it and hand it in before the expiration date. The ball was in motion. For so long this was only a dream. I hadn't realized how long it had been but as I was completing the application, I found certificates for classes that I had taken 20 years earlier to become a licensed childcare provider. I was amazed with how God was putting this together. If He didn't do anything else, I would have still been amazed, but God was not done yet. Oh no!

As part of the application process, all applicants were required to attend an orientation to learn what it meant to become a licensed childcare provider and get an understanding of all the regulations involved to determine if the childcare business was really for them. My orientation was scheduled for June 18, 2014. Having initiated the process in the past and having friends who were doing childcare I was familiar with most of the information that was reviewed. One thing that was stressed in the orientation was the requirement to have two egresses. That was non-negotiable. I left that orientation that day somewhat deflated. I thought oh well, I guess that's that. You see, I lived in a high ranch. I had the top floor, and my landlord had the bottom floor, but I had only one egress. The thought came to me that I could convert the window in the dining room to patio doors and add a small patio and stairway that could be used as a second egress. What would that cost? Would my landlord even allow it? He was supportive of my opening the childcare business, but I wasn't sure if he would be okay with me doing such major work. I thought for sure this would be a deal breaker.

The next day, June 19th my husband and I went out to dinner. While at dinner I explained to him what was said at the orientation and my ideas for creating the second egress. I told him that I was a little discouraged, but I was going to believe God. A part of me wanted to go to that familiar place of disappointment and discouragement but there was something on the inside that wouldn't let me quite go there. David responded that he would believe God with me. We continued to enjoy our date and did not mention it again that day.

The very next day, I *happened* to run into my landlord in the driveway. He inquired about the status of the licensing application (as I mentioned, he was supportive of the idea). I explained to him the problem of not having two egresses and my bright idea to create the second one (at my own expense, of course).

He made a face and said, "Hmmm, I don't know about that." Before I had an opportunity to become discouraged, he continued, "But what do you think about taking over the whole house?"

My neck snapped and I said, "excuse me?"

He went on, "Yeah, what if I moved out, you could take over the whole house, do the daycare downstairs and then you would have two egresses."

I wanted to scream but I was dumbfounded, and I had to maintain my cool. "I'll have to discuss it with David, and I'll get back to you" I responded.

"Okay, cool" he said and went on his way.

I could not wait to get into the house so I could scream! As soon as David came home, I recounted my conversation with our landlord. He just looked at me and shouted, "What?!" He was just as astonished as I was. Now you KNOW that must be God! Who offers to move out of the house they purchased so that their tenant could start a business? WHO DOES THAT! This man is not even a Believer, but God was using him. Isn't God amazing?!

Once David and I got our composure, we had a conversation about how this would work. How would it affect our finances, our family and everything else that comes with making a major decision. My husband was supportive and in agreement with moving forward. After having a conversation with the Landlord to say we were interested, we worked out all the details and planned to move forward. His plan was to move out early fall and we would use downstairs for the business. The application had been submitted to the state. What appeared to be an "obstacle" was eliminated, and we were moving forward. This licensing process can be a long, tedious process. There are so many documents, certifications, inspections, floor plans, and regulations to follow before one can be granted a license to do childcare. One of the inspections required is a visit from the Fire Marshall. My appointment was scheduled for mid-July. On the day the Fire Marshall arrived, he looked around outside and inside. He asked his questions and gave some suggestions and shared some experiences. However, at the end of the inspection, he turned to me and said that he could not approve me to move forward. There were two stoves in the house and our Certificate of Occupancy was for a single family dwelling. I explained that the current occupant was moving out and taking the stove with him (smile). He informed me to call him once that happened and he would come back give the "green light." Okay, a little disappointing to hear but not discouraging right? I mean he was moving out and then we could proceed. We could continue with our planning and preparation.

After much prayer and consideration, the business was given a name: Special Treasures Childcare! The business name was registered, the LLC formed, the Tax ID obtained, we were on our way. In the beginning of August, around my birthday *(something about August)* Linda, who would become my mentor, called and said she had "some things" to give me to help me start the daycare but I would need to get a box truck to pick them up. I was so excited. We arranged to meet on Saturday, August 9th. My family was giving me a birthday barbecue that day, so we arranged to meet early evening. She told me all I needed beside the truck was someone to load the truck. I thought, *no problem, what are husbands and sons for?* In the early evening as our guests were leaving, we all headed off to Linda's childcare facility. Once there we were told where to park the truck for easy loading. I had no idea what she was giving me, but I was grateful for whatever it was. Special Treasures was a step out on faith movement. I did not prepare and save for years to start this business. I simply went with the flow, the movement of God as he guided and directed me during the process. So, anything that I received was something that I did not have to purchase or try to figure out how to purchase. I was GRATEFUL.

As we stepped inside, I asked if she could give them a tour since they had never been there. As we went around the facility I could see in their eyes the same amazement that I had when I first saw it. That got me excited because I wanted them to have the same vision I had for what Special Treasures could be and the level of excellence that I wanted to establish. As we went around the facility she was explaining the changes she was making with new furniture and equipment in preparation for September. Finally, we reached the cafeteria and the end of our tour. Linda then turned to me, "This is everything I have for you to get started in your business!" My eyes widened in amazement, and I looked at David in disbelief.

"What! Oh my Gosh! I cannot believe it!" These words came tumbling out of my mouth and then I began to thank her profusely. Everything I needed. Changing table, toddler tables, tables, cots, cubbies, toys, dry erase boards, chairs, walkers, bouncy seats, a shelving unit, play yards, toys, toys, toys. As if that were not enough, she gave me several pieces of outdoor equipment. By the time they finished loading that truck we could not throw a marble in it! All I could do was give God the Glory. Everything and I mean everything that I needed to get this business started this woman GAVE to me. Again, WHO DOES THAT? GOD that's who! Often we go looking towards our own resources, the people we know, family and friends. Or we try to make it happen or feel we must be the ones to be the providers. But God will touch the hearts of people He chooses to bring what he wants to pass in your life.

It wasn't an easy road, and it did not happen in the time that I thought it would happen, but Special Treasures Childcare was born in my living room and dining room (not downstairs) on May 28, 2015, with my first child, Quintus McCain-John. It was not until November 2016 that the Landlord moved out and Special Treasures was moved downstairs; two years after the process began and 22 years after the desire was placed on my heart my vision came alive. Delay does not mean denial.

Jeremiah 29:11 (my favorite scripture, if you haven't figured that out by now) says, *"For I know the plans I have for you declares the Lord, plans to prosper and not to harm you plans to give you a hope and a future."* God knew in the early evening of August 6, 1962, that a 42 year old woman was going to give birth to a baby girl named Linda – me. Before that day He knew all the struggles I would have. He knew all the failures, all the mistakes I would make, the many disappoints and hurts I would experience. He knew the highs and the lows, the twists, and the turns and even the times when I would disappoint Him. But through it all He has had a plan for me. I have a hope and a future. My journey is not over. My story hasn't ended. Am I a kept woman? You bet I am!

To God be the Glory!

2
FULL CIRCLE

Ray Ramos

W hen God brings a man full circle it's not by accident. It's a process that embodies pain, anger, uncertainty, struggle, joy and finally completion. I can remember each feeling as I wear them proudly like stripes on a soldiers sleeve. I guess that is how Jesus must feel about the stripes He had to take for our salvation.

My story begins as I sat at the banks of the Euphrates River under the darkness of the night. The cool wind pricked xmy skin. At that river my mind wandered to my family back home. A rare moment of peace in a place torn by a chaotic war. The daydream was sweet, but it didn't last long. I remembered the months of physical and mental anguish and recognized quickly I was in the middle of war-torn Iraq.

That night, under a sky filled with what seemed like a million bright stars, I realized I didn't belong there and couldn't find a way out. So I did something I hadn't done in years, I prayed to God.

Within a few weeks, I was flown to Germany from Iraq due to an unexplained illness I was dealing with. After several inconclusive tests, I was sent to Fort Dix, New Jersey and finally to Walter Reed Military Hospital in Washington, DC. After a few months, the military declared me unable to perform my duties, and I was issued an honorable medical discharge.

I left Iraq with my life, and took the journey home to my family. After many years, I married a woman who completed me. We had three children and a newborn daughter who filled me with hope. As I contemplated my life and surroundings, I wondered if I would ever experience peace and understanding in being a man, a father, and a husband.

It had been decades since I turned my back on God in anger. My mother's unexpected passing caused me to have serious reservations about how God determined what was fair. Yet here I was physically and mentally worn, and about to make a decision that would bring me full circle – back to God. In that very desperate moment, I chose to lay everything down and ask for His forgiveness. I decreed that if He allowed me to return to my family safely, I would give my life to Him, and I would help other young men who had veered off course from His path. I would try to help them avoid the mistakes and pitfalls I experienced, and I would make it my mission to help them find success.

When I think back on that moment in Iraq, and the many crucial moments since then, I know with certainty that every decision I made led me to become the man I am now. Shortly after my time in the military, and the successful career I built as a New York City Police Officer, I pivoted and took the opportunity to begin work on a project where I could more directly serve the communities in need.

It was during that time that I began Project HYPE (Helping Young People Evolve), a non-profit program with the sole purpose of mentoring young men through their transition into adulthood. My early personal experiences and those as an NYPD officer led me to realize that there were serious gaps in their growth as a result of social, economic, and personal issues. The young men I encountered and ultimately worked with, lacked guidance, resources, and mentors who could provide them with critical experience. Creating Project HYPE allowed me to cater a program around their specific needs. It is a program that provides students with access to mentors with expertise in education, business, physical fitness, etc. Most importantly, the program teaches the young men that without God, direction, drive, determination, family, and commitment they will exist without ever realizing their full potential.

Project HYPE's curriculum is centered around four primary principles that reflect moments of growth in my life. When I now ask myself, how did I get here? And what kind of man am I? There are four clear answers to these questions:

I am a **strong man.**
I am a **responsible man.**
I am an **honest, reliable man.**
I am **true to myself.**

Strong
GROWING UP AS THE YOUNGEST OF THREE CHILDREN, I felt that my mother, Delores Steba, tried her absolute best to ensure that she spent quality time with me that she was unable to spend with my older brother Michael and my sister Mercedes. Her financial circumstances during their developmental years made it difficult for her to spend quality time with them due to her extensive workload. My mother, I affectionately refer to as "Ma," was determined to be there for me and as a result she devoted as much time with me as possible. Without a defined male figure in my life, she, as well as my grandmother, were the women who built my foundation.

My earliest memories of my mother included her tremendous

heart, compassion and love of family. She created baskets and treats for every child in the family and other children during the holidays. Her mission was to ensure that everyone felt welcomed, and it was evident in the way she treated those who visited our home. Through her actions, my mother taught me to be selfless, empathetic, loving and welcoming. It was at home through my mother and grandmother, Rafaela Haslip, better known as "Nana", that I learned the importance of offering a warm meal to those who sought advice or needed to vent especially during the holidays. I learned from them how to make anyone feel like family; welcoming the young and old alike to events where inclusivity was vital.

I modeled my character after theirs, knowing that my passion would be to seek opportunities to serve others in any available capacity for the rest of my life!!

Although my family was not wealthy, and we did not live, by any means, in the largest home on our street, I knew comfort and safety. With my mother and grandmother, I felt safe and loved, and in fact, lived a very sheltered life. My Nana, in particular, took care of me when my mother worked and often coddled me. I rarely traveled alone. I was not allowed to hang out in our neighborhood unsupervised, and spent many afternoons in my living room watching the latest television shows. My experience in the real world was limited by design. I was an overprotected child who lacked savviness and feared the thought of getting into trouble. It was an idyllic childhood.

However, as I grew into a young man, I began to make poor choices and desperately needed male guidance. The void of a consistent male figure meant that I lacked the specific knowledge that was necessary as I became a teenage boy and later a young adult man. My sheltered childhood meant that I had very few opportunities to overcome adversities. I had a few male figures in my life. My dad, Marcos, who was a factory supervisor, my uncle Norberto "Junie," who was an executive for the New York City Housing Authority and my uncle David – the godly man of the family who worked at the Metropolitan Transportation Authority (MTA).

I remember often feeling envious of the fact that my cousins had a "complete" family. They had someone whom they could talk to about manly topics and who could offer them guidance in all matters concerning males. As a young man in the hood, I was making poor choices in friends, work opportunities, and had developed a series of relationships that were leading nowhere.

During that period of my life I was desperately looking for a male role model. I needed guidance. I was fearful of new experiences, so after a failed attempt at college I decided to join the New York National Army Guard. My mother taught me to always self-assess, and I knew enough to understand that I needed discipline and leadership skills. I felt that the military could provide both. Excited, but unprepared for the reality of basic training, I could not have foreseen how quickly I would enter manhood. My drill sergeants instantly worked through the emotional issues I carried and they taught me to remain focused on the tasks I was assigned. It was in the Army that I learned about leadership and camaraderie as a Squad Leader. It was in the military that I understood how to persevere and work through any situation. I had to become accustomed to managing conditions that were outside of my control, executing complex tasks, and remaining focused on the mission. The experiences were challenging but rewarding. I was forced to learn to use my strength to get through to go to the next step. As a young man, I still did not fully understand what manhood was all about. I was now in my third year since joining the army as a young man, and I was learning through my military experience "how to man up." I still did not possess what being a man truly meant. To complicate matters, my first child was on the way and my mother, my rock, my compass, passed away.

To say that I was affected is an understatement. The depression that ensued was all consuming and enveloped me like a glove. I became angry that a woman aged 52, so young and so loving, could pass away in an instant and leave me alone.

I was desolate and lost, and it felt as if life had played a cruel joke. To add insult to injury, at her funeral the priest failed to mention the fact that she had a younger son or that I even existed, and additionally, my name was left out of the list of her children. The rage I felt grew, and for a long time, I shut down and withdrew from everyone, including myself. I suppressed all thoughts of moving on and drowned my feelings in alcohol and other substances.

I stayed hidden for a very long time. One day a light bulb turned on in my head. I remembered the training that I received in the military and hope began to rise in my spirit. The love and support from my sister Mercedes, my uncle David and my Nana helped to pull me up from the doldrums. Of course, I remembered the many lessons my mother taught me and I knew I could not disappoint her. All these factors helped me get to a point where I knew that immediate change was necessary.

Deciding to take a small step forward in a new direction requires inner strength. It requires determination, and it requires a vision. Over the years, my process for transitioning from one state of mind to another has not changed, and it is this message I share with the youth I teach at Project HYPE. As part of our curriculum, we teach our students about strength and the importance of forward movement. We use their personal experiences and our educational curriculum to offer them opportunities to overcome their fears, find inner strength, and to become leaders. The lessons on the inner strength that I learned from my mother and the military continue today as I draw from my training and the wisdom my mother imparted to me to lead others to change.

Taking Responsibility
THE LESSONS IN STRENGTH that I teach to my Project HYPE students wouldn't have any meaning if I did not also teach them to accept responsibility. Project HYPE students come from all walks of life, and although their circumstances are often complicated, it should not affect their desire to succeed in the present. Teaching them to recognize this is not always so simple, but I draw on my experiences to get the message across.

As I mentioned earlier, my family was not wealthy, I was raised in a very sheltered environment by women determined to protect me from almost everything. To help my mother, who often worked long hours, my grandmother took care of me and my siblings and instilled in us a desire to prosper. She made it truly clear that by taking care of us, she was ensuring that we would succeed in school. That was our only priority – to excel. Due to the lack of male role models, my childhood was primarily run by women. My dad, although around, tried, but lacked the consistency of pouring into my life and my uncles had their own families. My desperation to be "the man" led me to seek opportunities anywhere that would profile what I felt was manly. In high school, football became that outlet.

The football team's sense of purpose, camaraderie, and physical requirements would be the most rewarding aspect of the sport. It mirrored the elements I would find familiar in the military years later. The sense of a large "family" that I found on the football team was alluring; however, it also led to the beginning of my poor life choices. It was on the football team that I made my first set of unsavory friends; friends who did not value education but enjoyed fighting and whose mentality did not often mirror mine. A pattern developed, but my family was unaware. Daily I would "get jumped" by young thugs on the bus ride home from school. On the B12 bus, my faithful commute home, these thugs saw me as a threat and a nuisance. This pattern lasted a while, and without guidance, I resorted to taking matters into my own hands. I began to carry a small knife to school. This experience was the first of many choices that would alter the course of my life. I knew that I would need to take responsibility for my choices to move forward.

One bright morning, after getting jumped the day earlier, I pulled out the knife in my homeroom class to defend myself against another threat. This fateful choice brought me to the principal's office, where my father was called, and it was suggested that I transfer to another school.

My mother and grandmother worked hard to ensure that the school I attended was better than the last, and while this quick turn of events felt like undeserved punishment, I came to quickly realize that I had to accept responsibility for the way my life was turning out. Not speaking out and not alerting my family of the daily physical abuse I was receiving was a lack of wisdom and a lack of responsibility on my part. I am sure they would have helped me or offered wise counsel. My decision to address the matter in my own way led to my immediate transfer to a school that I did not want to attend. I found that I was disappointing my family and realized that a change was desperately needed. It was at that time that my family made a tough decision, and my uncle David intervened to help straighten me out. He brought me to live with him and his family. I saw this adjustment and change in my environment as punishment! In hindsight it was my uncle's way of balancing the heavy female presence in my life and to teach me what a real man looked like.

Upon finishing high school, I decided that taking ownership of my past actions was necessary for my continued growth. I knew that there were areas where I lacked sufficient knowledge and that I needed to surround myself with people who could serve as mentors in those areas. My decision to join the military was a direct result of assessing my past choices, taking responsibility for my current circumstances, and embarking on a path to change my future. It was the military that simultaneously gave me my first sense of freedom while teaching me about my duty to others.

As I turned nineteen, surrounded by my fellow soldiers singing happy birthday, and performed what felt like my hundredth pushup, I knew that I had made the right decision. I had searched within, taken responsibility for my choices, and embarked on a path to make a difference.

Being Good For Your Word

THE MILITARY FILLED ME WITH PURPOSE, clarified my direction, taught me to be disciplined and sharpened my skills. These life lessons were invaluable to me and I was able to easily translate these skills to begin a ten-year career with the New York City Department of Transportation. I had lost my mother, had two young children, and now I felt that I could honor her memory and be a good father to my daughters by helping others in that capacity. It was a complete shock when I was denied entry to the Department of Transportation because of a medical deficiency. The disappointment was overwhelming. I temporarily let the setback dictate my choices and spent several years walking down the wrong path.

By 1993, often high and using drugs recreationally, I experienced failed relationships, and was unable to properly deal with my young children. My military experience was not translating into the real world. In short, I was failing in so many areas of my life and I did not like who I was becoming. It was clear that my window for change was quickly closing. After my mother's death, my grandmother took over the role, full time, as a "mother figure" and a "moral compass" for my siblings and me. It was evident that I was disappointing her with my behavior. I did not know how to begin to change so that her opinion of me would improve. I knew that I could not enroll in school nor could I return to the military full time.

Internally I was hell-bent on getting it together, and while school may not have been for me at the time, the military taught me how to find focus and use discipline to pivot and start to change my life. I took a job as a meter maid and patiently waited in that role for ten years working hard and doing my best to ensure that I was learning. It was during that time that a friend told me about an opportunity in the NYPD as a housing police officer and helped me to prepare for the test. I firmly believed that taking this job would be an opportunity to make something of myself; I knew I owed it to myself and my family to succeed, and so I took the test and waited.

It was a fantastic day when I discovered I would get the opportunity to serve others in the capacity of a police officer. My acceptance into the police academy changed my outlook completely. I had been feeling incomplete and unsure of my worth, but my acceptance into the police academy meant that I could change my future and the feeling of accomplishment that I gained, as a result, began to alter my self-esteem. My graduation marked a turning point for me as my grandmother looked at me for the first time in years in a different way. She was proud of the change I had made in my life, she was proud of the discipline I regained, and she was proud of the man I was becoming. Her support and strength changed everything for me at that moment and gave me a level of confidence that propelled me to the next step. Everyone who was in my life, along the way, attended my graduation.

At the NYPD, I requested to work with Community Policing Affairs, where I would serve the public and have the opportunity to make a direct change. My role in this department directly influenced the work that I now take on as the Founder of Project HYPE. As a community police officer, I had to develop my public speaking skills to convey important messages to the members of the communities that I served. I had to develop empathy and compassion, and use my previous experiences to understand their circumstances, be more relatable, and to understand how I could better serve their needs. More importantly, I had to be consistent and good for my word. The community knew who I was and relied on me to help them keep their neighborhood safe. It's a message that we impart to all our students at Project HYPE where we utilize our lessons and their initiative to drive home the importance of being good for their word.

Staying True To Who You Are

MY JOURNEY HAS NOT BEEN LINEAR and required many abrupt turns that threatened to derail my ambitions to succeed, but there was always one thing that kept me going – my faith in God. Even when, in times of great pain, I stopped praying and speaking directly to Him, God always heard me, kept me safe and showed me the way. I credit the Lord for the opportunity and ability to serve the young adults in my program today.

As a grown man and father of four children, there was a time when I still felt very lost. I was promoted and working with a wonderful unit within the NYPD, and had finally found peace at home, yet I was restless and incomplete. Ever present in my mind was the belief that I was not special and did not have anything unique to offer. As I had on that night by the Euphrates River, I once again prayed to God to help me, not knowing that this simple act would lead me directly to the ministry.

Shortly after, members of the church I attended suggested that I participate in a course to become a minister as they had seen me speak to the teens at my non-profit. I had been preaching to them about the importance of school, good character, and the positive impact of being decisive. The pastors at my church felt that the message that I gave my students, the passion that was always a part of my speech would be powerful when used to deliver the word of God. Without a second thought, I decisively embarked on a journey to become a minister and to share God's work in my life with others.

When I look back on the questionable decisions I made as a young man, and the heart-wrenching moments I experienced, I see God's divine hand working to make me relatable to those I now help. My challenging experiences on the streets, the lessons I learned in the military, the pain and instability caused by my mother's death have all provided me with opportunities to share my story with the young men I meet every day who do not see a way out. It's much easier to understand now how God's plan had to happen in a particular order to prepare me for the much larger tasks I now face. Although my time in the military provided me with a specific set of skills, it was my position in the NYPD that allowed me to learn how to translate those skills to serve my community. It is now my time, as a minister, that helps to weave God's message in everything I say and do.

One facet of the work that I do with the young men in the Project HYPE program is to help them understand that they are special. We work to translate their experiences into unique opportunities for growth. It was a lesson that was difficult for me to grasp as a young man myself, but I have found that for me to value the unique services I provide to others today, was necessary for my particular journey. Our journeys are how God makes us one-of-a-kind and uniquely qualified for our missions in this world.

Conclusion

PROJECT HYPE EXISTS AS IT DOES TODAY because of all the hardships I experienced as a young child, a young man, and later as an adult. It is structured to guide young boys through their own unique set of difficulties and provide them with the tools in an educational setting that allows them to become strong young men. Our program does not seek to change our students' personalities, their home environment, or try to sever their connection to their communities in order for them to succeed. What we hope to impart to them is the fact that despite possibly encountering negative influences in their neighborhoods or at home, and despite any negative traits they may have developed, they hold the key to their success and can completely alter the course of their future.

When I began the program, I knew that I would need to create a curriculum around the four characteristics I developed, and so we tailored our educational curriculum to highlight them all through the program. We teach our students first to find the strength to persevere and work through their difficulties and emphasize the natural growth that occurs when they cross over to the other side. The next phase of our program focuses on teaching them the importance of accepting responsibility for their actions, their current behavior, and for the path they have chosen. This stage allows our students to set new goals and helps them embark on a different path. After their acceptance of responsibility, we teach them to stay true to their word. If they are unable to remain steadfast in the promises they have made to themselves and others, there is no possibility for real growth. We find that in our program, this lesson, in particular, requires a more significant time commitment and so we have created several educational curriculums that help our instructors guide our students through this specific step. Lastly, we work with our young mentees to help them stay true to themselves. We emphasize the importance of finding their purpose and how to translate that in the real world. Our mentors work with each student directly to ensure that by the time they transition to college, they are confident in who they are as a student, as a young man, and in what they can offer this world we live in.

As I write this chapter, I know that I have a long way to go on my journey, and I treasure this phase of my life. When I am not running Project HYPE's weekend program and attending field trips with our students, or when I am not writing this manuscript for my indented book, I focus on my work as a minister preparing sermons and helping others within the congregation. This beautiful season of my life is filled with promise, new people, new challenging experiences, and a renewed sense of hope. As a young man, it was hard to imagine a life so full of happiness and possibilities. Because of the hardships I encountered, I am now able to help others every day. I want to spiritually touch every person with whom I come in contact, and to impress upon our youth their unique value. I have indeed come full circle.

3
PAINFUL REALITY

[Donovan &] Jennifer Freeman

10-9-21

I grew up in Jamaica with ten brothers and sisters, so it is quite an understatement to say that I came from a big family. My upbringing was characterized as extremely humble. Although we did not have much, my family prided itself on education, hard work and commitment to family and God. So even though there were many times in my childhood where I was left feeling uncertain as to where life would lead me, my strong faith and family values cemented my preparation and determination for whatever challenges that would come my way.

My older sister was pursuing nursing, and my Uncle Frank admired my mother's commitment to her family, this prompted him to file for all of us to come to America. This is where my journey would take an unexpected turn. While I never had any aspirations of leaving my small hometown, I knew I had to embrace the next phase of my life. So, one by one my siblings migrated. At eighteen years old, I was left behind to patiently await my turn. But without the support of the people to whom I was accustomed, I was left feeling alone, scared, and unsure. I kept thinking and asking myself, *"What will the future hold for me?"* Well, I soon learned that it would include a man named Donovan.

Donovan and I met four years prior. If you ask him when his life started, he will undoubtedly answer, "The day I met Jen!" We met in school and around sixteen years-old, we had developed an amazing friendship and connection. However, when we graduated we lost contact with each other. To our amazement, we met years later at a school reunion. The bond that we had was reignited and I later gave birth to our beautiful daughter, Latoya. While Donovan knew I would soon be leaving Jamaica, he often recounts that this left him feeling sad, but optimistic; that someday he would reunite with his family. A year later that is exactly what happened! I returned from the States, we got married and I filed for him to come to America. We were now going to start our family and live the "American Dream."

Soon after we gave birth to our first son, Dane, who ironically was born nine months to the day that Donovan came home. Needless to say, I was happy to see my husband! Dane was our "love child." Few years later we continued to add to our family and I gave birth to our last son, Bryan.

As parents, it was always important for us to raise our children in the church, so that they could have a strong spiritual background. We enjoyed family time on Sunday afternoons and really bonded with our children. At the time we lived in Brooklyn, New York, but were planning to buy a home in Queens. We were working hard and our dreams for our family continued to be actualized. Our family took trips to Disney World, went on vacations for spring breaks, enjoyed movies, activities, and quality time. Donovan enjoyed being a father. He grew up without one, so he didn't have an example to emulate. However, he would often say that he found an ultimate Father in God. God certainly did call Donovan to be the man, husband and father that he was. Our family was blessed; we knew that as long as our children were happy we were complete.

Latoya was a sweet child. She was a dad's dream of a daughter. Donovan would often daydream about the day he would proudly walk her down the aisle. I remember giving birth to her, I was giving birth to my reflection, my little me. Our bond was unbreakable. I remember sending her photos of things that I would think she would potentially like, when I went shopping. She would do the same with me. I was her mother, but I looked up to her, I confided in her, she was my best friend. My daughter loved nursing and modeling, she loved children and most importantly she was so happy.

DANE WAS OUR LOVE CHILD. Donovan was elated to have his first-born son. He would be able to pass down and instill certain core values to him. Dane loved playing basketball. Most of all he loved to laugh and enjoy life. He would take the shirt off his back for someone in need. Dane also loved his bun and cheese! Dane would tend to stray, but Donovan would lovingly redirect him. Because Donovan grew up around an unsupportive environment he was able to identify with those who were negative influencers. Donovan would share those stories with Dane as a precautionary measure. Although they didn't always see eye to eye, he knew he could always come to his father, who would love and protect him. He was always encouraged to accomplish his dreams and desires in life. Dane followed his sister and wanted to pursue a career in the medical field.

Bryan is my youngest child. He is quiet and very reserved and shares his father's personality. He does not like a fuss, he would rather be in the background and never have the spotlight on him. When he was born, I would call him my "Chocolate Baby" because he was the darkest child in the hospital. He loves to read and expand his knowledge. Bryan has an unspoken way of commanding people's respect. He is kind and loving. He graduated from college and has a bachelor's in business and administration.

You see, we had the perfect family, beautiful and happy children, and a loving and peaceful home. But one Saturday in May shattered it to pieces. I woke up to an incredibly beautiful day as we were invited to a 50th Birthday party for a very close friend. I took care of a few things around the house and about noon I left for the beauty salon to have my hair done. The kids were left home with Donovan and he, as usual, would prepare breakfast for them. Saturday mornings was a day where we would all relax and sleep late. Dane enjoyed watching basketball on the sports channel, Bryan would have the cartoons on, and Latoya would be cleaning her room and listening to music. After I came home from the beauty salon, I learned that Dane was home all day, in the living room watching sports and of course eating his bun and cheese.

Dane greeted me in my room as I was getting dressed. He said to me that I was beautiful and was inquiring about my whereabouts for the evening. "Mom, where are you going?"

I responded jokingly, "To the same place you young people go on Saturday nights!"

We both laughed. Looking across the room, he turned to Donovan, "Pop, you look nice." We all laughed and Donovan said thank you. I looked at my son, and he looked handsome. He was dressed nicely and his hair was cut immaculately.

"Where are you going, son?"

"I am just going to a BBQ," he responded. I told my son to just be careful, he said that he would and that he loved me. That night Dane left for the BBQ not knowing that we would never speak, kiss, nor embrace each other again.

We went to the birthday party and it was beautiful. We got home at about 2 A.M. and got ready for bed. Dane was not yet home, however, that was not alarming as it was Saturday night, and we knew that young people stayed out late. We settled down for bed and just as I was falling into a deep sleep I heard the front door bell ring. I thought I was dreaming, but it rang again. I awakened Donovan and he went to the door. Immediately my thoughts went to Dane, it was now 2:30 A.M. and he was still not home.

"*Oh God,*" I thought. I was lying in bed for about five minutes and Donovan still had not reappeared. I began to get worried, so I jumped up, put on my robe and went to the front door. Just as I appeared in the doorway, Donovan asked, "Where is my son?!"

With a trembling voice, I echoed, "Where is Dane?"

The friend that he went to the BBQ with started to say, "Mom, I don't know how to tell you this."

I interrupted him, "Where is Dane?!"

"There was a shooting and Dane got shot and he is not coming home."

I thought to myself, *"What do they mean my son is not coming home?"*

I began to scream, and Donovan was on the stoop crying, begging for his son. "Oh God this is not happening!" I kept repeating those words in my mind. I wanted it to be a dream. I didn't want this to be my reality, how could this be happening? I later learned that Dane and six other people were shot and he was now dead. Hearing those words made my head spin. I could not believe this was happening. I started walking up and down the street in front of my house in pure shock. My son Dane was gone.

Our life after that became even more complicated; we had to endure the long process of finding the people responsible and a trial. It was truly a journey and our trust in God is what got my family through what was an extremely hard and painful time in our lives. Dane did not deserve what happened to him; he was a happy and respectful young man; how could he meet such a fate? It took many years before they arrested the man responsible for his murder. After a long and arduous trial, he was convicted of second-degree murder and is serving 25 years to life.

Our son Dane will never be with us again and that hurts. He had dreams that will never be accomplished. His death was extremely painful to his sister Latoya as well. It was hard saying goodbye to Dane, little did we know that we would soon lose another member of our loving family.

A few months after her younger brother's untimely death, Latoya began to cough. As a baby, she never had any health problems – not even as an adult. Her brothers suffered from asthma, but not Latoya. She was strong. So when she began to cough we didn't think much of it. Probably just a cold we thought; it will pass. One month turned into 6 months of coughing. By this time she had seen her primary care provider and pulmonologist. She was diagnosed with asthma and placed on inhalers and steroids. However, nothing worked. She would get so short of breath she couldn't even walk at times.

We started to get worried. She went into the hospital several times with multiple chest x-rays and they were all normal. Her health started to decline, she started to become lethargic and began losing weight. She started to lose faith that she would get better. She got so ill one night she could barely breathe so we took her to the hospital again. Finally they took us seriously. The thought before was, why would a 29-year old relatively healthy woman have anything but asthma? However, they quickly rushed to get a CAT scan for her struggling lungs. When the doctor came into the hospital room, I was sure he would just say everything is normal, we just need to change her medication. That unfortunately was farther from the truth. For some reason when doctors give you bad news they always lead with "So." That was the first of many "So's" that I would hear leading up to the final "So" that tore me to pieces. It was a tumor, the doctor said and they did not know what, where or why. Latoya could not make any decisions as she could barely breathe let alone talk. They ran so many tests and yet no answers.

A biopsy needed to be done to see if it was cancer. I called my niece who is a doctor to help us make the decision on what to do. We decided as a family and the medical team to transfer her to a hospital in Manhattan that would be able to better care for Latoya as they had a bigger intensive care unit and doctors who were aware of Latoya's condition. We transferred Latoya to the new hospital at night. I remember the lights and sounds as if it were yesterday. Latoya was lying on a stretcher with me and her cousin surrounding her. She looked scared. I was scared. By this time it was even hard for her to talk. When we arrived at the new hospital they rushed us to the intensive care unit and a team of doctors and nurses met us.

I felt relieved, I was certain they would cure her. The doctor let us know that Latoya could no longer breathe on her own and that she would now need a breathing tube to help her. This meant she would be asleep and no longer able to talk to us. My heart sank. My baby, my first born, my only girl on a respirator – this could not be real. Her cousin asked her if she wanted them to do everything for her to save her life and she nodded yes. That was the last decision she made on her own. They gave her medication to sleep and the doctors put in the breathing tube. Seeing her for the first time on the breathing machine was so surreal. She was finally resting and not struggling to breathe but it was heartbreaking nonetheless. The next several months felt like an eternity. They decided they needed to do a biopsy to see what this tumor was. We found out that the tumor was wrapped around her heart and the main blood supply going to her lungs. It was squeezing the life out of her – no wonder she could not breathe. How long was this tumor growing in my baby? Why didn't I realize something was wrong before? So many questions running through my head. The night of the biopsy, I rubbed her feet and kissed her cheeks so that she knew mommy and daddy were there with her. Her father and I never left her side. Our life was spent in the hospital with our daughter. I would rest and go back. I would read scriptures to her and pray into her spirit. I never gave up hope, no matter how bad things seemed to be.

WE WERE THERE EVERY DAY TALKING TO HER so she knew we loved her, and I knew she felt the love. When they came out of surgery the doctor came to us and said they were only able to get the biopsy but could not resect the tumor. The next morning we found out Latoya had a stroke from the procedure and that her brain was swelling. They had to remove a piece of her skull to relieve the pressure on her brain. They placed the skull in her abdomen so that it would not die. She could not move the entire right side of her body. They decided to try chemotherapy to shrink the tumor, but that ruined her kidneys and now she had to be on dialysis. During all of this the doctors attempted to wake her up as they were now going to give her a tracheostomy, so at least she could be awake during all of this. Finally two weeks after they put her to sleep she was awake. But she was not the Latoya of before. She had a stroke, part of her skull taken out, and she lost a tremendous amount of weight. But thank God she was awake! We spent the next couple of months just waiting for a breakthrough. But with every step forward, we had two steps back and a lot of "So"s.

"So, unfortunately Latoya has pneumonia and her lungs are worsening."

At this time, Donovan became ill and had to be hospitalized in the same hospital as Latoya. He was diagnosed with sciatica. Bryan was left alone and had to always come home to an empty house. What a trying time for our family.

On December 31st I left Latoya after spending New Year's Eve with her. We didn't even make it home before we got the call.

"So, sorry to let you know that Latoya's heart stopped and we tried everything we could, but she was too weak."

My baby, Latoya, was gone.

"God, why did you take another child of mine?" During that whole process I wanted so desperately for everything to be alright. I thought for sure God would come through for us. We just lost our son, Dane 15 months earlier. All I had to do was to tap into my faith in God; I know he wouldn't let us suffer again. God, "What are you doing?" Here we were still grieving. We did not know how to even begin processing the grief of our son and yet had to deal with the death of Latoya. But I heard a voice in my spirit telling me that, somehow I would come through. I was not going to allow this to defeat me and my family. I remembered the night when they returned her to the room after removing her skull. I asked God to give me a breakthrough. I couldn't bear seeing my daughter in that state again. I was angry with God for allowing my son to die. But then I remembered what happened to Job. If God allowed it then, I knew that I would be able to overcome it. God did not heal her body, but he did heal her soul. Latoya came to accept God as her personal Lord and Savior before she passed. Although she couldn't speak, she managed to tell me that when she was released from the hospital she wanted to be baptized.

My faith was strengthened despite all that I had gone through. We cannot give up on God, because God will never give up on us. He is sovereign and good. His ways are always higher than our ways. Donovan and I knew that even though what happened to us was so devastating we still had to put our trust in God. Peter said to Jesus, "Whom shall we go?" Who else can you put your hope and trust in but Him. I have learned that He always comes through even if its not the exact way we expected. I found that the enemy would have me question God and myself. At times I thought I was being punished for something that I did. God's purpose had to be fulfilled. I said to myself, "God gave them to us as a gift," and I have no regrets with my children because I love them and that has kept me.

I remembered the days of being overwhelmed with the news of Dane's murder and having to go through trial. We had such a good support team, which was imperative. Even more so, we learned that no man is an island, no man stands alone. We are our brother's keeper. Everyone we came in contact with came with a sense of love. Today when I speak with people, they say that I am such a strong woman. I say that it's not by my strength alone, but by the strength of God. I met a lot of angry mothers who have hate for the person who killed their child. While I had anger, I didn't allow hate to seep in. I couldn't harbor hate, because I needed a light spirit in order to move on with my life and family. I still had to be a mother to Brian, and wife to Donovan. God kept me in the right mind, and for that I am so thankful.

God heals broken hearts; He gives peace to the troubled and hurt. I learned even more that happiness is a state of mind, and I was happy with my relationship with God, my husband and my son. Even in the midst of my pain, I knew God was keeping me and I know He will never let me go.

Two years after Latoya's death, my mother passed away. My mother felt my pain when I lost Dane and Latoya. She loved her grandchildren. My mother also buried two of her children. We shared this pain in common, a pain no mother should bear. Everyone was hurt by their passing. Brian, is still devastated, but doesn't talk about the situation. Donovan helped our family to stand firmly on the Word of God.

Donovan would say to others, "Remember, whatever you are going through it's just for a season. The loss of a loved one, a broken marriage, whatever it is, they are things that come to test and challenge you. It is part of our DNA, you will never escape challenges. There is still an awesome God who is sovereign and all you have to do is tap into him. He will not give up on you."

Because we are Christians it does not make us exempt from trouble. We will have tribulation, however, our faith and trust in God helps us to overcome: The pain is real.

4
A GLAMOROUS LIFE

Lisa Ray

My plan at one point was to be the next Diana Ross, but being in a male-dominated music business, I quickly lost that desire; and instead wanted respect as a businesswoman. I achieved success to a degree as a comedy promoter, and finance professional, all while battling insecurity but displaying confidence. Even when I was not so sure of my actions, I heard my father's voice saying "never let them see you sweat." You see, I had a level of confidence when it came to business, in fact, I was a person known to "make it happen!" Ultimately realizing God was keeping me and preparing me through each trial. He never left me and I have to say, I've cried many nights asking God to relieve the pain and also asking God to please forgive me for thinking I could ever fix anything. Only He can. I am equipped to endure and fulfill what God has for me because He has been preparing me all my life. It is ironic that the very gift the Lord gave me of writing poetry at seven and eight years old, I've now returned to as an adult in my fifties. Through that same writing ability, poetry, God speaks to me and uses it to bless those suffering, experiencing a trial or trying to continue to brave their journey. God is blessing me to be an encouragement, inspiration, and motivation to those on the verge of giving up. But all glory to God. In my flesh, it is hard so I must trust God. I lean not on my understanding. Remember I am more than a conqueror and I am fearfully and wonderfully made. I have a made-up mind to serve the Lord and share His goodness with others.

Overcoming to Becoming

EACH DAY I RISE GIVING GOD ALL THE GLORY for another day; and as I put one foot in front the other, I look to hear from God for His ultimate wisdom. I am in pain each day, but pushing past it for His Glory. There are some days I feel overwhelmed, but I pray for His power and trust Him in my suffering. God is revealing my healing. All adversity is a step closer to what God has for you. What do I mean by that? What doesn't kill you makes you stronger, just like pressure creates diamonds. Never in a million years did I think I would have a child to raise on my own – but God. Losing my dad who was my greatest inspiration, I thought I would die.

I spent eight years in pain and suffering without a diagnosis;

enduring test after test, MRIs, EMGs, and more just to hear we don't know what is wrong. Wondering if I would die, how sobering is that thought? Losing friends or people who I discovered did not have my best interest at heart. That is a huge hurt and let down. In God's word I am reminded, in Psalm 118:9 ESV, *"It is better to take refuge in the Lord than to trust in man."* In my time of reflection I heard from the Lord, and He told me He was with me and would never leave or forsake me; moreover, in my heart I knew He was preparing me for a great work my whole life and now I'm about to take flight. Habakkuk 2:2-3 ESV reads, *"And the LORD answered me: 'Write the vision; make it plain on tablets, so he may run who reads it. For still the vision awaits its appointed time; it hastens to the end--it will not lie. If it seems slow, wait for it; it will surely come; it will not delay.'"*

I wrote the vision and made it plain that I would be an author. In May 2018, *Angel's Heart Guided by Light* came to life as a published book of poetry.

Although I've been broken, it has allowed me to grow closer to God. He has strengthened me in my hard-place, in my trials, feeling inadequate and alone; my God pulled me out of the muck and mire to stand tall and confident in Him, the Lord Jesus Christ!

So here I am today, determined to make the good choices to

be the example of love, patience, and suffering by overcoming and claiming victory of Jesus in my life.

I am still battling, faced with slings and arrows of the devil, but no longer looking at the situation, instead looking and seeking God even more than ever. You see, I get it. Once you know you're His, you know you have already won! Don't get me wrong, the biggest struggle for me is patience, which is a fruit of the Spirit. It is also directly linked to faith. Think about that, hmm, I have faith and I trust God. According to James 1:4, *"But let patience have its perfect work, that you may be perfect and complete, lacking nothing."* This is my test that I must pass and I will not fail. My God is working it all out for His Glory.

Every day in pain, sometimes feelings of sadness, wanting to cry, believing I would feel better afterwards! But today God said, "Lo, I am with you until the end of the earth." I have survived because of my God, and although there are scars, mentally I am stronger, physically reminded of my humanity, but better because of the power of God dwelling in me. Who am I? I am a friend, a daughter, a sister, a mother and a believer of Christ determined to live for Him!

I often question people's notion of me. They all want to know what she is. Is she white, does she have a husband, dating anyone? Is she happy alone? "Just keep going Lisa," I said, "God has a purpose and plan for your life." Even when

God's people try to block you from using your gifts, "I will make room for your gifts," says the Lord. A lot of my pain has been at the hands of people who say they love me. I'm looking for the revelation, action, show me, don't just talk about it.

Becoming a Mother

AS I DELIVERED MY SON, I gave birth to a Prince. It was at that moment that my life forever changed. At that moment, I felt such love, warmth and comfort. I felt the love of God; it has to be. The way I love my son in my heart is the same love God has for us! Raising my son was such a joy, and contrary to what many may think I became a lot more conservative. I'm a mommy now, responsible to nurture, love and guide this young life to become a successful, productive life. But how can I do that, you ask? I'm not sure, but what I know is I would raise my son to know Jesus, and in doing so I was confident he would be okay and we would be okay. Today my son is a grown man on his own journey to be a true servant of Christ! This place is quite different because I'm always his mother no matter his age! I find it especially hard, because I raised him and that part is now done. I raised him to know God. The foundation was laid and my work is done. I have to trust that God's purpose will come to pass. I feel like I'm continuing my own journey again with patience and a test of faith.

I Had a Feeling

JUST WHEN YOU THINK EVERYTHING IS GOING GREAT life happens! I was at the peak of my career on Wall Street earning a six-figure income, raising my son, paying tithes, bills, traveling and being able to purchase virtually anything I wanted – within reason. After a fabulous vacation in Montego Bay with my son, I returned to work. It was a Monday morning. As I sat at my desk, I proceeded to initialize my desktop computer and nothing worked! I realized today was the day, and then the phone rang. I checked the caller ID and it was Human Resources. They had eliminated my job, and I remembered that just before vacation, I had written at least eight procedures and steps sheets on how to create several reports for the heads of businesses. This left me feeling like they played me.

Actually, I felt relieved because after the market crash of 2008, for two years I saw people being laid off and fired on the spot. Everyday someone else was missing from their desk. Even if *you* survived, the person next to you was let go and *they* had a family, bills, issues and dreams. So, it affects us all if someone is suddenly canned! By the time I was laid off, I was experiencing stress at a record high and felt I could not trust corporate America!

The year leading up to being laid off, I had sprained my ankle and it would never heal. I'd seen so many neurologists, podiatrists, specialists etc., and I was never diagnosed. I repeatedly had issues with my balance, numbness, ringing in my ears and bouts of dizziness. I spent years wondering if I was dying. Was this because of my indiscretions during my younger years? "God, am I dying?"

Immediately, I made important doctors appointments to make sure I was okay, and ironically discovered a lump on my left breast that required surgery and a biopsy! Two weeks later polyps were discovered on my womb and needed surgery number two. Both surgeries were benign, but this was only the beginning!

Fast forward two years later – it would stop me in my tracks. Excruciating pain which further affected my ability to walk. I was never hiding. but I felt vulnerable and often unsafe. I went from wearing 4-inch heels to being barely able to put on a shoe. I have a "drop foot" and after a misdiagnosis, a back surgery that I should not have had. I suffered over 20 falls in a one-year period, slurred speech and suffered in pain, ultimately receiving a diagnosis of multiple sclerosis. Multiple sclerosis is a debilitating disease where your body attacks your immune system. For me it affects my mobility, ability to walk without stumbling, falling, heaviness in my legs and excruciating pain.

This was difficult to say the least; my son was now in college and I was struggling to make sense of this diagnosis. The dream of my son graduating college was in jeopardy! I put it in God's hands and I knew Bryce would graduate and the Lord would make a way!

I often felt like an outcast among friends, family, and even in church. What happens if one of you is sick? Let the elders pray! Not only am I a single parent, but I am sick, fatigued, and barely able to buy food! Jesus said he will never leave nor forsake me. God, I need your help, please help me.

All my life I was popular and very shapely, I might add. I was the cute little Black and Puerto Rican girl with thick, long hair. I received a lot of attention from family, friends, and some people who had inappropriate thoughts about me. How did I know? There would often be older men offering me fur coats, money, whatever I wanted. But my dad taught me not to accept everything from anybody. As a young girl, getting attention from the wrong people made me feel very self-conscious. I tried to hide my shape by always tying sweaters or jackets around my waist; this way no one could see the hourglass shape; I did not want anyone looking at my behind!

I dreamt for a guy to like me for my personality and see my heart; besides, I was good person. I would think, *"Stop looking at my body, I hate it and I know I'm fat. Gotta lose weight."* But Daddy made fried chicken, cabbage, with white rice! I couldn't resist. Daddy cooked, and I cleaned my plate, and as always, there was room for seconds.

As a Black and Hispanic girl growing up in the sixties, the world was still divided. I quickly faced experiences with prejudice even among my own family. A cute little girl with pigtails and a freckled face. Sometimes I resembled my peers, but most often I did not! You see there was something different about me that stood out. With my Puerto Rican family, my color was like theirs, but my hair was bushy and didn't quite lay down like my cousins; no, my hair didn't blow in the wind and fall back in place. If the wind blew, I better have a hat on! One thing I remember is that my mom would take her time doing my hair using products like Suave, Vitapoint, Wella Balsam, or Tres Flores oil. On Easter, mommy used a rattail comb, water, and dippidy doo to make beautiful Shirley Temple curls, and my hair was gorgeous. Mommy's sister, TiTi Mary, always showered us with love and gifts. We were her baby sisters' daughters. Now, my Black relatives were loving and kind as well and they truly accepted us. Growing up in a black neighborhood, we ate traditional southern dishes like fried chicken, collard greens, and macaroni and cheese. That was no ordinary fried chicken. It was the best, made by my dad. My daddy cooked so well that my mom would let him do most of the cooking. He was a chef, our chef, but also one in the army. He really enjoyed cooking and I believe it brought balance to his life being a police officer; it had to be therapeutic. Those dishes grandma made were recreated with Daddy's special touch. Don't get me wrong, we looked forward to seeing Abuelita in Spanish Harlem too, because there we would have bacalao, pasteles, and arroz con gandules – deliciouso!

As I grew, I became more shapely but I hated my body; I thought I was fat and extremely insecure. I did not think I was pretty and I thought everyone wanted to have sex with me, but I would avoid it at all cost. No sex before marriage or you'd be considered fast, not respected, and I wanted respect.

I am planted and ever growing in this refining process called life! Dying to self enables you to bear fruit and live life. I get it now and my Lord has answered my prayers. You see, He has been preparing my entire life for purposeful work for His glory. Even though many times I may have been in a hard place, a dark place; holding on by faith, knowing and believing in my heart that God has a great work for me to do. Despite making so many mistakes and thinking I'm in control. As I reflect on the accomplishments, experiences, people in and out my life, heartache, sickness and disease, I see God has been with me through it all. He is my strength, power, love, grace, mercy, peace and joy! This is for His Glory. God is changing me inside and out and suddenly doors are opening and people and opportunities are available to me to spread the Word of God in a way that all can relate. I am now overcoming adversity by seeking God and trusting the process. *"It is good for me that I have been afflicted; that I might learn thy statutes."* Psalm 119:71 KJV. I was constantly being prepared even during the inadequacies I felt in my childhood.

Being so curvy as a young girl meant that an older man might date a teenager! Case in point: I dated a man, who was maybe 26, and I was 18 and very inexperienced, but I followed his lead. He ended up on drugs pretty bad and although I did drugs too, it was a social thing and I was able to quit and walk away. God spared my life during that time, and then I met my first love, an NBA basketball player. He invited me out five times before I said yes. What's the worst that could happen? I'd have a nice dinner and never have to see him again! Well, that did not happen, I fell in love! We traveled, spent almost every day together, even dressed to match; the doorman thought we were married. Then suddenly his routine changed, and he said he was going out of town for a day! I felt in my gut he was lying and guess what, I had the keys to his place. I said to my dad, "I know someone's there, I can feel it! I'm going out there!" And my dad talked me out of it. He said, "You don't want to do that, Sugar!" So, I listened to Daddy. It made sense, he wanted to protect his little girl. A day later, I showed up to his place and there were two neighbors there who quickly left when I walked in. They were scared. I walked into the bedroom and saw a picture of his ex-girlfriend from college. She had been there, and it devastated me. I thought staying with him would keep him away from her and because she didn't live here, his feelings would stay with me. Right? Wrong! I didn't trust him and my heart broke. Was I not good enough, pretty enough, sexy enough, smart enough? I was not willing to put up with just anything! Totally devastated, it took me two years to get over him. I really got over him when I met another guy who showered me with diamonds, took me to work and picked me up. He wanted to marry me – he really loved me. That too ended!

OVER A PERIOD OF EIGHT YEARS I experienced slurred speech, numbness by my right rib cage, and my equilibrium was off. I saw a multitude of doctors including neurologists who ordered MRIs, EMGs, biopsies, etc. According to the test results I was fine on paper, but my body told a different story. All I know is I am surviving a story of pain, weakness, and often a broken spirit. One of the most frustrating things was the back surgery that I should never have had. You see, a few months before I saw a podiatrist for my "drop foot" and he insisted it was coming from my back. They sent me to a spine specialist who told me if I didn't have surgery on my back, I would be crippled. Really. I pushed that to the back of my mind and several months later while out doing karaoke with a friend, I suffered excruciating pain and could not stand up straight. The next day, unable to walk, my friend took me to the hospital. I spent 5 days in the hospital and lost 17 lbs. Now I had screws and rods in my back and it made things worse. Afterwards, I fell over 20 times in one year! *"What is going on? Am I dying?"* Considering I was never diagnosed with anything, I had to get to the bottom of this and sort things out. Finally, I gave a PA (physician's assistant) an opportunity to review my symptoms, and yes take more tests, including bloodwork, more MRIs and a spinal tap. Lo and behold, they discovered they had misdiagnosed me! The test showed I had 12 bands revealing Multiple Sclerosis! Unbelievable. From that point on I saw a specialist at Weill Cornell with medical records in a binder 2 1/2 inches thick. After a thorough review, I was officially diagnosed with Multiple Sclerosis (MS).

MS is a disease where the immune system attacks your body and can debilitate a person physically or cognitively. Multiple sclerosis (MS) is an unpredictable, often disabling disease of the central nervous system that disrupts the flow of information within the brain, and between the brain and body. For me it's physical, and it affects my mobility; I walk differently, and everything has changed. I suffer from weakness on the entire right side of my body. I used to love to roller skate, but it's not safe for me because my balance is off. Running is also out of the question, because my gait is no longer fluid and I wear an AFO brace on my lower right leg for support. Truthfully, this sometimes makes me sad and I do not get many phone calls or invited out much. I think people feel that I am needy and don't want to be bothered. Thank God I can still drive and have some independence. People need people, and it's amazing how I've helped so many people, and now today I find myself alone. Friends who I thought would be there for me are not! But God sent angels: people who I never thought would consider me, and for that I'm grateful, I'm thankful. What I've learned in this trial is that God wants me to completely rely on Him!

God Has Spoken

CLEAR AS DAY, GOD SPOKE TO ME AND SAID, "I told you long ago I have something for you. Did you not believe me? Well now walk in it and see the truth! The victory comes to you through vision, so walk in it, and in fact pursue it. Watch how I use you to bless others with the gifts I have given you. Know it, believe it, and see it. Know I Am the giver of life and I have a purpose for your life. To follow laws is great and it's good, and you will do a good thing as those who trust me.

All that I have allowed to happen is for My purpose in your life. I Am in total control; continue to trust Me and have faith knowing that I Am the potter and you are the clay. I have cancelled every plan of the enemy against your finances. The plan against your family including your mother, brother, sisters, and son has been cancelled. Your health will be restored and the court decisions will be reversed in your favor. Decisions in government agencies are reversed in your favor. You will live and not die; you will stand for holiness and righteousness! No weapon formed against you shall prosper. You will speak to large audiences, as I have given you in a vision many years ago. Your book was published and completed for My Glory. I Am sending people who will help meet every need. Move forward with College Connect, I gave that to you. Trust, knowing, I Am preparing you for greatness in Me for My Glory! I created you and the plans I have for you will move forward and be completed with my power and authority. Trust me and be still when I tell you to seek Me in all things, for all things; all your decisions and concerns."

Surviving Normal

WHILE GROWING UP IN JAMAICA, QUEENS, I always felt loved by my family. My mom and dad made sure my siblings, and I were safe and secure. Everyone treated me special, maybe because I was the baby. Mommy would make breakfast and dinner. We had lunch at school. She would comb my sister Maria's hair daily; no doubt because it was fine, smooth, and shiny! Maria's hair was easy to manage. As for me, it was a different process. On our block we had several families with kids, and for a time we were among the younger ones. We played hide and seek, stickball, punchball, football, and of course my favorite skully. It was a big deal to play in the street. When you could play in the street you were growing up; it was a sign of maturity … so I thought!

Why, as children, are we so inclined to do what grownups do, or get to that next stage of development? I remember telling my mom that I had to get the white wedding dress, then my brother's friend Demetri would marry me. Silly wasn't it, to have a crush? But I was a little sister to him, a cute little girl. It was unblemished like how the simple innocence of the time was. In school I had a pretty good experience, even remembering when my first-grade teacher Ms. Sarota picked me up for school on my birthday and bought a cake! Boy, those were the days. I got to celebrate my birthday with the whole class. I also remember being chosen for a special assembly to recite a poem that I wrote for Congresswoman Ms. Shirley Chisholm. I won the schoolwide spelling bee and always received excellent grades.

For me school was a very positive experience, both socially and educationally. I loved to learn and soaked up everything like a sponge. I had great teachers who were concerned about the children and that made us want to be in class doing our best. If you were disobedient, you could spend time in detention. No one wanted to be in detention and be labeled as a bad kid; so we strived to do well.

My mother was a very beautiful woman who doted on her children; buying my sister and me the finest clothes with matching bags, hats, gloves. And do you remember the muffs? You couldn't tell me anything! Although three years apart, my sister Maria and I would often have matching outfits like we were twins.

My dad did most of the cooking and it was always fresh vegetables, meat from the meat market with a starch, you know mashed potatoes, pasta, or rice. We ate a lot of rice, and my dad made a mean Spanish rice and he always tried to speak Spanish because my mom was Puerto Rican. That was hilarious!

On Saturdays we had a big breakfast as a family. Oh how I looked forward to Saturdays. We would have everything from corned beef hash and biscuits to fish and grits. Daddy also gave us special treats when we ate all of our dinner. He would buy us Snickers bars, and ice cream with the cones. He made everything seem so special. Every week we would get a delivery from the soda man. My favorite flavors were grape and orange soda. If I remember correctly, there were twelve bottles of soda, different flavors that came in a case; and when the doorbell rang, we would peep out the window then run to daddy and say the soda man is here, all excited!

Daddy worked as a cop at a Manhattan South and a Brooklyn precinct. Daddy always drove a Cadillac. He never had a brand-new car, but it would be gently used and he took great care of it, just like he took great care of his family. Mommy was a nurse and she was beautiful, very sweet and kind. Mom worked throughout the week, and sometimes on the weekends. On holidays, she would buy my sister and me the cutest outfits, complete with fancy tights, laced dresses and beautiful ribbons for our hair.

I remember once our whole family was on the front page of the Daily News. Mommy, Daddy, my sister Maria, my brother Anthony and I were spread out on the daily news when Mayor Beame was in office. My dad received a citation for taking down criminals in a local bar while off duty. My family on the front page dressed in our Sunday best, guys in suits and gals in fancy dresses with gloves and curls in our hair. What a nice memory, I still see that moment.

I eventually graduated from elementary and moved on to Junior High School where my daily routine was getting to the handball court at 7am to hold it down for my friends. Playing singles and doubles, I was on the winning team. My second year in middle school I ended up in 7-SP, which I believe stood for "Special Progress"! The teaching in the

SP program was accelerated, and geared toward children who were gifted and talented. These programs allowed students to cover grades 7, 8, & 9 in two years. It excited me to represent my community and my family. I was the kid who didn't need any help with my studies or projects. I continue to excel, completing the SP program in the 9th grade and moving onto High School.

In High School I was determined to play basketball on the girls' team. Honestly, practice was very disciplined with Mr. Asher. We ran suicide plays and others to prepare us to be champions. I enjoyed playing, but not as much as when I played with the fellas. You see, the fellas taught me how to play full court. I kind of lost the passion for playing basketball with the girls. Of course, I was the only girl on the team running down court with big hips, so much so I received several nicknames: "little miss big hips," "legs," and "hips ahoy." Yes, now I'm self-conscious because someone always drew attention to my shape. I was a little girl in a woman's body.

Giving Up Control
TO HAVE CONTROL IS TO HAVE THE POWER to run something in an orderly way. The verb control means "to be in charge!"

So, I was raised to be confident in who I am and in my abilities. I always had the natural ability to assess a situation and come up with a quick and efficient solution, from when I was about the age of twelve years old. I sometimes complained that I did not understand why as the youngest of four siblings, I was given so much responsibility. As I grew older, and at this point trained, I realized my dad saw that I was the responsible one and would eventually be the family member in charge. In charge of making sure we all had life insurance when my dad died. Making sure the taxes were paid, house maintained, handling mommy's health concerns, helping my siblings and never letting our credit go bad. The problem was, I was never taught how to deal with my feelings. *You are strong Lisa, you can handle it.* If I showed emotion, then I was weak and people would take advantage. Well no one was going to take advantage of me, so I thought. I believe even when we think we have it all together, we all are vulnerable in certain situations and find ourselves dealing with emotional issues and having to navigate through life. *Put on a good face Lisa, you are so smart.* The truth of the matter is I've been broken inside, riddled with insecurities and trust issues. Lord knows I do not want to be played and I don't want to be hurt! I only recently realized that I never had a chance to understand the emotions I was feeling. I did not know how to handle them, always feeling like I was being judged and not loving myself enough! Well I love myself and I am beautiful; God made me this way and He is in control. When things don't go as expected, I sometimes cry, pray, and try to take a step back because it's God's plan and not my own. I am releasing the pain of insecurities and disappointments, and trusting God in the process. He's working it all out for my good, and I'm learning and I am better at giving up control with God's help. Cast all your care upon Him because He cares for us, He CARES for ME!

Experiencing Loss

THE YEAR WAS 2016, WHEN THE STRUGGLES I FACED would change my life forever. After being diagnosed with Multiple Sclerosis in February, I was scheduled to get my first treatment on March 23rd, which was the day after my 50th birthday. Never would I have ever imagined struggling to walk. The weakness on my right side affected me from my shoulder to my toes. My ankle and foot had limited mobility, but the use of the AFO brace gave me the support I needed to walk with a smooth gait; although I could not use it when I wore shoes. I tell you not being able to wear shoes was a challenge. So, I looked for sandals that had a supportive strap with embellishments so I could still be fancy, besides, I used to rock a pair of high heels. I don't miss heels as much as I miss just putting on a cute flat. My goal is to walk without the use of the brace and without using a cane, not necessarily in that order.

A few months went by and I had three treatments of Tysabri under my belt. Tysabri, like all other MS medications, slows down the progression of the disease; there is no cure. Well there is no man-made cure, but God has the cure and He is a healer. I kept myself busy working at Nyack College and doing Praise and Worship at a sister church. Both kept me motivated and encouraged. The week leading up to July 4th that same year, my family on my dad's side said we were having our first family reunion. I was so excited and looking forward to meeting more family. The blessing was, I had already traveled to Georgia the previous year and met many family members. In fact, a whole lot of us celebrated my 50th birthday at a fabulous seafood restaurant; three of my best friends came as well. Days before our scheduled family reunion my mom was rushed to the hospital and would spend a month in intensive care. My sister and I, along with my Bethel Gospel Tabernacle church family, began to pray. In fact, Deacon Armand made several trips to visit my mommy, Ophelia, in the ICU and we would pray, sing worship songs and continually speak life. Mommy had visitors: her only grandson Bryce, Titi Mary and Carlos, her nephew and niece Raymond and Norma, my sister Maria and brother Anthony, and his childhood friend Clifford. Everyone deals with seeing people in the hospital differently. Mommy's body was swollen and they put her on dialysis, which was extremely difficult. You would hear her scream, but we continued to speak life and believe in God. Sometimes my Aunt would say, "Oh my poor sister," and immediately my sister and I would tell her no, do not say that, speak life. Mommy is going to be okay. We believed and that was our prayer. Eventually, the swelling in mom's body subsided, and she went to rehab. Mommy came home on dialysis, but one Friday after she returned home from treatment, mommy passed out right in front of me and I started praying and singing. At the same time my brother called 911 and they told him to put her on her side, and she came to. That was a close call, but she ended up going to the hospital; but guess what? Mommy's kidneys recovered and she was taken off dialysis and would not go back on it ever again! Thank God, that was truly a miracle! Hallelujah!

Mom would have many more hospital stays over the next three years. The stress caused me to start falling and I ended up on disability again.

My beautiful mother would continue her fight to live, constantly calling on her savior Jesus Christ! She would say, "Jesus, Jesus please don't leave me," and for certain as much as she suffered, she was an Intercessor prayer warrior praying for everyone, from the members who often served her communion to the nurses, CNAs, and doctors who took care of her. Whether you were a neighbor or a friend, she prayed. She prayed for children and the unborn child; she was an angel doing the work of the Lord until her passing.

I would often go see mom at the rehab where she was learning how to walk using a lower limb prosthetic. She was such a strong woman and she never complained. It hurt my heart to see her in pain. It broke me down many times, oh how I love my mother. I would take her outside and play the music of familiar artists from the 50s and 60s and I would show her videos. We would sing together and I often played gospel music and scriptures for her. It was soothing and peaceful. One day I was about to leave for work and received a call from the rehab nurse that mommy was not responding. When I arrived at the rehab, EMS was working on her. I called out to her, "mommy," and immediately she opened her eyes. Knowing she was responsive made me calm and I knew I had to stay with her. My sister and I were at the hospital with my mom, and we prayed and constantly told her we loved her. I remember on the fourth day in the hospital I was able to get her to eat soup, drink Glucerna, and drink water. I spent about 5 hours with her and I figured mom would become stable and come home. However, the next morning the doctors called me and said her kidney and liver were failing. I immediately contacted Pastor Sherrod so the prayer warriors would seek the Lord. That Sunday, I went to the 11am service because I needed to mentally and spiritually be prepared. We celebrated the birth of Jesus, as it was three days before Christmas. I heard the Holy Spirit say to me that mom would be there when I got there. On the way to the hospital, I called my TiTi Mary, Mommy's sister, my son Bryce and my sister Maria. Deacon Benjamin and Sister Angie visited mom, shared scripture, prayed and sang songs of praise. Eventually my family was all there, and we figured we would just stay there, so my son and sister went to buy dinner for everyone. After about 10 minutes the heart monitor started beeping and Mom's oxygen level was compromised. We called out for the nurse and doctor. When the nurse arrived to check my mom's sugar level, it was down to 14! Oh my God what's happening? I immediately started praying and singing songs, even the nurse started singing praises. The doctor ordered an injection of sugar, and when they did that my mom looked at us and turned her head. I kept singing "Oh the Blood of Jesus," and I hugged my mom and prayed in the spirit in her ear, and I looked at my mother's face and watched her take her last breath! As hard as it was, it gave me peace to be with her. You see, I prayed to God that when he was ready to call her home to please let me be there to hold her hand because I did not want her to be alone. The Lord honored my prayer. I called my son and told him he must come right away. He was already on the way, and when he arrived, my aunt and I were distraught with heartache and crying. Bryce hugged me as my sister walked in and proceeded to break down, and I said, "go to your aunt and attend to her." Eventually, my son walked away to be alone. We called my brother Anthony to see if he wanted to come to the hospital, and like we suspected, he did not want to see his mother that way. We hung around for two more hours, during which time I consulted with Pastor Sherrod who gave me numbers to call and direction on how to proceed. Then my family and I all gathered around my mom, prayed together, hugged and kissed her as we said goodbye. My mother was truly an angel on earth. She exemplified the love of Christ to all she came in contact with. Her sweet demeanor and gentle spirit always saw the good in people; for those who struggled or were broken she would say, "We have to pray for them," and she always spoke life. I'm thankful that I had a mother in my life into adulthood. I know she is with our Lord and Savior Jesus and we will be reunited one day in glory.

Finally Living in Purpose

WHAT DO I DO NOW YOU SAY? Breathe. I never took the time to breathe deeply. I think that I've had some sort of anxiety all my life. Take the time to breathe in and out, relax in the process while releasing stress, pressure and pain. In your calm, stay focused on the Lord Jesus Christ and concentrate on His name. In His name there is power, so breathe!

For the past few years I've been working part time in education, published a book of poetry *Angels Heart Guided By Light*, maintained a blog on my website angelsheartsforhope.org, and wrote a play "Life Is Poetic." I've been invited to speak at churches, the public library, and performed the play at least five times. God's message of love shines through, and the challenge of having Multiple Sclerosis, yet not giving up on oneself, correlates with Jeremiah 29:11, *"For I know the plasn I have for you, plans to prosper you; plans for a hope and a future."* I am determined to be a visible witness for the Lord, through sharing my message of hope and overcoming adversity in my testimony. God makes the impossible possible, so trust in the Lord with all your heart and lean not on your own understanding, in all of your ways acknowledge Him and He shall direct your path. This road that I am on is Spirit-led and I was finally able to open a business called ANGELS HEARTS FOR HOPE FOUNDATION Inc., to encourage those suffering with disease not to give up on themselves, but to seek God and live their lives on purpose. I am more than a conqueror and I give all glory and honor to the Lord as I seek to share the truth of the gospel while encouraging others that life is not over because you have a disability. The truth is there is a disability in all of us, and we need the Lord to live life "In Purpose."

5
TWISTED

David Anderson

The year was 1958. I was home watching my father holding my baby brother Sydney. Sydney was barely breathing – you could hear the congestion in his lungs. That night my parents took him to the hospital. The next day my mother woke me up and told me that he passed away. It was a shock to me; it was the first time I experienced death and pain. It had such an impact on my life that there were times when I dreamt of his funeral. My mother told me that the hardest experience for parents, in this life, was to bury their child. I never forgot the pain in her eyes or the pain that I felt.

This story is for the person who is in pain and does not understand why. Especially the person who has trouble reading and does not understand why. I was once like you. I understand what you are going through but know that I am praying for you. You are not alone. There are many other people like us. Writing my story is extremely difficult for me to do.

Dyslexia is defined as – a general term for disorders that involve difficulty in learning to read or interpret words; but does not affect general intelligence. Albert Einstein was dyslexic. Many people who have difficulty reading, experience pain because they do not know why they struggle with what comes so naturally to other people. There are more than three million cases of people in the United States who have been diagnosed with dyslexia. I lived for 40 years and didn't know I was dyslexic. I found out that it is a neurological condition also known as a reading disorder. I also had difficulty speaking. When I would speak the wrong words would come out and people thought I was trying to be funny. I was not planning to make people laugh and their laughter was hurtful. So, to hide the pain, I laughed along with them.

I am a man who understands panic. When I panic, my brain moves too fast and causes me to stumble over my words. I have to force myself to slow down so that I can catch my breath.

At the age of eight, I remember having to repeat the third grade. I had a teacher who was very mean to me. When it was time for me to read out loud, I would become anxious, and I would always get stuck on a word. It was not because I did not know the words; I knew the words. I had a hard time reading them out loud because in my brain I saw the words in reverse order. Believe it or not, I am better off sometimes reading things backwards than to read something forward. Sometimes I would read the second word in the sentence before the first word.

I will never forget hearing my 3rd grade classmates laughing at me. I was told by many that I could not read. That was painful and I took that as truth. I felt small. Sometimes people may say something to you and about you, negative or positive, and it sticks to you for life. Emotionally, I would shrink. Just writing this chapter, I had to use my phone and Google 90% of the time just to check the spelling to make sure I had the letters in the correct order. It is the little everyday things I sometimes still struggle with in reading. So, the Lord is helping me, not only to talk about this, but to go one step further and write about it. Most people are embarrassed to talk about this. I am an overcomer.

Getting back to the third grade. My teacher would beat me like a slave. She was an old white woman and I knew she never liked me. She would use the pointer stick and beat me with it. I can still hear the stick cutting the air when she would beat me. Between the beating and the kids laughing most people would have lost their minds. I tried my best to brush it off and act like it didn't affect me.

MY TEACHER WOULD ALWAYS GIVE ME A NOTE to give to my parents about my behavior, they would sign it and then I would get another spanking at home. To escape the pain, I turned to alcohol at an early age. The first time I drank alcohol I was maybe 11 or 12 years old. It was a can of beer. My parents had a West Indian background and they did not play. Do not get me wrong – my parents loved me and they were good parents. When I became an adult, my father told me his father was abusive to him; he left his home at the age of 16. I kept to myself in my teenage years. Funny, when I was 14 years old, my parents were worshipping at Westbury Gospel Tabernacle, a branch church of Bethel Gospel Tabernacle (our mother church). There were no children my age at the Westbury church. I complained so much to my mother that she asked Sister Gertrude Caesar (wife of Bishop Caesar, Sr.) if I could join the Youth for Christ Choir. She said, "Yes." I was happy to be back in Bethel again – you see, our family was raised in that church before moving to the Westbury fellowship. One Friday night, I got a ride from someone, who will remain anonymous. We were driving to church and the person who was driving asked me, "Do you smoke weed"? I said, "Sure". Little did they know it was my first time. From that day forward I was curious about weed.

I was young and eager to know more about drugs. Of course, I was told not to use drugs. But I was fooled by the enemy.

I started out with weed and alcohol. Then I graduated to harder drugs like crystal meth. By the age of 20 I stopped going to church, because of my cocaine use. Think on this for a minute: I did alcohol, weed, pills, uppers and downers, cocaine sniffing, all in a day. I would call it getting "nice." It took away the negative feeling I had about myself.

I lost 20 years of my life. I was married at twenty and I had a son at the age of 21. Because of my drug use I was divorced before I was 25. My first wife could not stand my drug use. I would get so high by drugs she would say, "You were better off drinking." It was cheaper. I continued getting high every day. I was a train wreck going fast every day. The problem was I had no brakes. I could not stop getting high. I was a functional addict. I would always go to work and be there on time. I would work hard during the day and work just as hard getting high at night. I would stop getting high at night when it was three in the morning. I had to come down from the high to get up and go to work at 6am. I worked 6 days a week. Some nights I would party with people from my job. They would get sick and could not make it to work the next day. I would go to work; I would look sober. It was a lifestyle for me. Some nights I would get cleaned up and put on a nice suit and some great looking shoes. I would go out to a club or to an upscale, high-end bar. I would "play" with everybody in the bar. When I was high and well-dressed, I forgot that I was dyslexic. I would be able to talk with people and hold a conversation. Alcohol became my "Liquid Courage."

AFTER A WHILE I WAS TIRED of living like that, I needed a break. I was not happy anymore. I will never forget this kairos moment in my life. One night I went to a club in the city (NY) and while I was sniffing cocaine, and drinking cognac, the Lord asked me, *"Are you having fun?"* He blew my mind. I knew it was the Lord after all that cocaine and alcohol. God spoke directly to me, because He is greater than all those devils – even the big ones: cocaine and alcohol.

Shortly after that I ended up back at my parent's house because I had to move out. My sister came to me and asked, "Do you want to be free?" She said, " Let me pray for you." As soon as she prayed, she said, "Lord, I want my brother back." Lena called out every demon that was in me. I started to walk upstairs to my room and before I could get to my room the Lord was dealing with me. I was not high anymore, I was crying. I cried out to the Lord to forgive me. I really wanted to scream. My parents were in their room and I did not want to frighten or alarm them. I realized I was in the presence of the Lord. What came out of my mouth was the 23rd Psalm, "The Lord is my Shepherd. I shall not want alcohol, cocaine, or the street life. I surrender to you Jesus." I used to have my cocaine delivered to me at work. The next day when it was delivered to me, I told my friend I do not need that anymore, he looked at me strangely. As I gave it back to him, I said, "I don't do that anymore because the Lord saved me." I was working in the junkyard at that time. I went to the back of the yard to worship the Lord. Before I knew it, I invited the eight men from the job to church.

I was serious for the Lord then and now. I am even more serious for the Lord now. In Christ I am living proof, there is hope after dope. John 3:16 *"For God so loved the world that He gave His only begotten son that whosoever believes in Him should not perish but have everlasting life."*

"Lord Jesus, I pray for the many who are suffering and in pain. I pray for those who turn to drugs, alcohol and other addictions believing that these substances would help their pain. Lord, you are the only pain regulator. Help them, if they are reading this book, to turn to you instead of the bottle or the drugs. I also pray for those who may be struggling with dyslexia, not knowing that it might be dyslexia. Lord, I pray for those who are in pain – emotionally and mentally because they do not know they're suffering from dyslexia in Jesus name. Amen."

6
LITTLE MESSENGER

Ana Harris

In 2012 my relationship with God had gotten to an amazing place. Before coming to Christ, I lived a life that pleased me and my fleshly desires. Having a relationship with Christ, my desires changed. I joined the church choir, I was active in ministry with the youth church and I made a decision to abstain from sex until marriage. I was so serious that I had gotten off birth control. I was fasting. I was waking up early to do devotionals and sometimes staying up late to journal and pray as well. My then boyfriend, now husband, Steven, had also started to come to church more often as well. But it only took one time to produce a pregnancy.

One day I was at choir rehearsal and I had gotten lightheaded. So lightheaded that I needed to sit down. The choir director made a joke and asked if I was pregnant. I chuckled, smiled and said no but in the back of my head I thought,

"AM I PREGNANT?" Two weeks later, a pregnancy test and ultrasound confirmed I was indeed going to have my SECOND CHILD! Was I surprised? Not really. I sort of set myself up for that to happen. I certainly was not anticipating another pregnancy – a second time out of wedlock. All I could think about were all the people who were going to judge me for making the same mistake, TWICE!

Nevertheless I persisted. I kept going to church and I told the people who needed to know. I was so disappointed with myself for not keeping my promise to God, but now I had a bigger promise to keep. That was, to raise two children who would know and love the Lord our Father. As ashamed as I was I didn't let what anyone said about me stop me from being the best mother to my children. I worked full-time as a medical assistant at a Podiatrist office and I had a two year old at home. My boyfriend, at the time, worked as a tattoo artist and we lived in a room. Literally we lived out of a bedroom and only used the bathroom and kitchen when absolutely necessary. It was definitely not a glamorous or ideal place to raise children but for us it was better than being homeless.

Ideally the plan was to save up enough to get our own apartment but with student loan debt, low credit scores and rent increasing every year it was humanly impossible for two young parents from New York to get on their feet to find stability with one toddler and one baby on the way. My boss had given me a dollar raise about two weeks into my job because I was such an excellent employee. At the time thirteen dollars an hour seemed like so much to me. I was able to pay for little things here and there but in my heart I yearned for a better place for my kids to experience a better upbringing. Steven had taken a UPS job to add a little more income to the pot as the nine months were rapidly approaching. Like my first pregnancy I was diagnosed with Hyperemesis Gravidarum at one of my prenatal visits because of excessive vomiting. As the months came to an end I was experiencing excessive swelling, headaches and episodes of high blood pressure like I did in my first pregnancy, but the hospital refused to diagnose me with pre-eclampsia. At 20 years old I was probably viewed as just another young black girl on Medicaid who didn't know what she was talking about but I knew what I felt and it felt like I wasn't being taken seriously. I would try to schedule the appointments while my daughter Sarai was at school. Steven was at work for most of my appointments or he would drop me off and head to work. I worked up until I was 8 months pregnant.

If that wasn't enough to stress about during my pregnancy the doctor who owned the office I worked for passed away of lymphoma when I was about 5 months pregnant. It was so uncertain what would happen with the only three employees he had. Eventually the practice was sold to a podiatry group and they said I would be promoted to office manager. I was given the responsibility to interview someone and hire them to temporarily take my place because I would be going on maternity leave. Supposedly my position was secure but to my surprise, they ended up hiring an office manager right before I left. To a much, much greater surprise I was fired, via text message, by the same office manager they hired a few days after going on maternity leave. They had me transition the office and handle all front desk training maintaining patient contact just to tell me they no longer needed me, VIA TEXT MESSAGE! Now I was out of a job, but I did qualify for unemployment for about 6 months. I had enough time to be at home with my anticipated baby boy with some limited money coming in on my end.

I started going to appointments weekly because we were at the end of the pregnancy. I remembered going in for an ultrasound and the technician said something that I kept hearing my entire pregnancy. "You're measuring bigger than you're supposed to at this time." Of course I asked what that meant and again my questions were blown off or minimized like nothing was wrong. So being young and naïve I didn't push for them to explain it further. At my last appointment before Micah's delivery the Nurse Practitioner (NP) also said the same thing. At that point I was worried and annoyed that every medical professional that had me under their care was not explaining what that meant.

Did it mean I needed a C-section?
Would I have to be induced?
Was my baby in danger?

ON DECEMBER 2, 2013 at the conclusion of one of my checkups, the NP left the room and when she returned, these were her words. "You are going to have the baby tonight!" I immediately called Steven and told him that I was going to be induced. I could tell that something was up with Micah's heart rate as the look on the NP's face was one of concern. They called for transport but it took some time because they said there were a lot of women already in labor and delivery so they needed to wait for a room to clear up.

As I waited my worry increased by the minute. I called my mom to pick up my daughter and I waited for my best friend to come meet me at the hospital. Steven was at work, pretty far in Long Island, so it took him a while to get to me. The process of being induced took a while anyway. I had a love hate relationship with the medication, Pitocin, that night. It started off really gradually but then the nurse realized that it was too much for me so the dose was lowered. They offered me an epidural and I said, yes! But I later realized that only one half of my body was numb. Concern overwhelmed me. Firstly, the worried look on the nurses faces as they checked our vital signs. Secondly, my lingering feeling of uncertainty and last but not least my questions being pushed aside. All these factors created an air of unease for me!

A resident and an attending Labor and Delivery OB/GYN came in to talk to me very briefly. I told them about my experience during my first pregnancy and that I didn't want to be constantly checked, vaginally, by several different residents. The attending physician told me that they were a teaching hospital and nothing more. I was alone, in pain, and worried about Micah. My blood pressure was elevated so I was not about to argue with them.

As the delivery progressed, Steven and my best friend, Elizabeth came and the waiting game began. The lovely resident and attending physician came in again to check on me. I told them that I was feeling pressure and may need to start pushing. They told me to hold off to wait because they didn't have enough people on staff to do an emergency C-section! I tried my best to hold off and to be strong but after a while I couldn't take it anymore. I started screaming at the top of my lungs. At that point the room became full of nurses and doctors. I had everyone's attention. I told them that I had to push right then. So they prepared me to start pushing. It seemed like I was pushing for about an hour and I felt my energy getting lower and lower with every push. I felt dizzy, weak, and my head was pounding. The pain was indescribable. There aren't words to express what I was enduring.

They kept telling me I needed to keep pushing so I made one last push and he was out! I was so happy that it was all done and I finally had my baby boy. I felt like I was in another dimension. Time was still for a while. I didn't know what was happening because the doctors all rushed him away and crowded the bassinet. Steven and Elizabeth went to look at him and I was on the birthing bed. I wanted to meet him but I knew I didn't even have the energy to hold my arms up. My body was cold and I was trembling but at that moment I was just thankful that I didn't need to go through a major surgical procedure.

They seemed to be working on him for a while so I assumed that they just needed to be sure his heart was okay. Stephen walked over to me and he also had a weird look on his face, like he knew something was up. I didn't question it at the time because I was physically, emotionally and mentally exhausted. Finally they brought him to me wrapped up like an overstuffed burrito. I was enamored instantly. He looked like he had been through a lot. The feeling of not doing enough to get him out sooner was creeping into my mind. His face was so swollen that he resembled a mini Asian Sumo wrestler. His left eye was blood shot red and in my head I thought that in my moment of wanting to give up I had hurt him. I was so weak I couldn't even sit all the way up to hold him. They didn't leave us with him for too long before taking him for the rest of the night. I didn't see him again until the next morning.

When he was brought to me there was a notice on the bassinet that read: DO NOT SWADDLE ON THE LEFT SIDE. So when I asked the nurse what happened she said a doctor would come to talk to me about it. I didn't un-swaddle him or move him around too much out of fear that they would blame me for something I had no idea was happening. I waited for doctors to come and when they did I was alone. The doctors told me he had Erb's Palsy and was paralyzed from the shoulder to wrist. They said he had suffered a birth injury and they had to take him in to get X-rays to make sure his arm was not broken. When I finally opened his blanket and took him out of the swaddle his arm was limp, lifeless and bruised up. It looked like someone had given him birthday punches. He was swollen all over from all the trauma during the delivery. He had only been in this world for a couple of hours and he already met struggle, trauma, pain, inequality, malpractice, injustice, and neglect. The only thing I could do was pray. I prayed in the most authentic way I knew how at that moment. I was angry, scared, worried and disgusted at the way they mishandled our son. He didn't ask for this. I had asked on several occasions why they kept saying he was measuring bigger than expected and no one told me he was too big for the birth canal. No one warned me that he would be at risk for something like this. I couldn't comprehend why in all those years of medical training not one person thought to treat me like I mattered or like my child's life mattered. No one cared enough to explain or have the right conversations. They didn't even take the time to explain what it meant to have Erbs Palsy. They just told me and left the room. They said his pediatrician who had never even had a conversation with me before his birth would be in to explain what it meant.

The pediatrician told me that his paralysis may not resolve. That he would need to have physical therapy and follow up with several doctors to keep up with his progress. They said he might not ever swim, play sports, tie his shoe, or use his left arm for anything. It was possible that he may get some movement but it wasn't certain that he would. My 20 year old mind could not handle any more struggles. In a matter of four months I had to deal with four life changing experiences such as death, sickness, loss of job and unstable housing. It just didn't make sense to have to deal with so much at the same time. It wasn't fair and I wasn't shy about telling God how I felt. I had to let it go or I was going to start to hate God for making me struggle so much. We had asked to speak to the doctor who delivered Micah but she never showed up. I wanted her to see the pain in my eyes, I wanted her to take her job more seriously, and I didn't want her to hurt any more children. She needed to see what she did and take responsibility for it. She owed us an apology.

We were discharged with no further instructions on how to care for his injury. No follow-up with neurology or orthopedics. They couldn't even tell me exactly what was wrong anatomically. They didn't know what nerves were damaged or what to do to make him better. I left the hospital with no hope for him. We reached out to our church family and they prayed, our family visited and prayed with us and for us. I was not hopeful. I was on autopilot and I was just going through the motions. The silver lining in all of this for me was that at least I had been fired and was receiving unemployment so that I could stay at home and help him heal. When we finally settled in at home that day I started to do research. I found some Facebook groups for parents of kids with Erb's palsy and I started to look up ways to make it better. When I called to make an appointment with physical therapy they denied me an appointment because I hadn't received his insurance card and wouldn't receive it for 2-4 weeks. I started to do physical therapy myself. I wasn't about to wait around for his nerves to wither away. We needed to create muscle memory and build up his strength.

I cried when they told me he wouldn't be able to get an appointment. They caused this damage and now the very hospital would not grant him access to care because he didn't have a piece of plastic to cover the ridiculous amount of money it was going to cost to fix him. I could feel myself falling into a depression that was going to be my mental downfall.

I was overwhelmed with trying to make sense of why it happened. I thought maybe if I pushed harder he would have been ok. Maybe if I was more persistent in my questioning it could have been avoided. The truth was that none of it was my fault and I asked the right questions. I was home with him for two months before he was able to finally get physical therapy through early intervention; a program that provides services for young children who have developmental delays or specific health conditions.

When our pediatrician saw us for the first visit he indicated that Micah was definitely going to need services. By the second visit he still had not gotten to a physical therapist because we still hadn't received his Medicaid card. When I explained that to the doctor he gave me the most unsympathetic answer. "Time is of the essence, what are you waiting for? You should have already started." I can still remember holding back the tears after telling him they denied me services at the very hospital where he worked. All he should have said was, "Well, what are you waiting for?" And my answer would have given him clarity. Nevertheless, he sent me to a social worker and I thought to myself, *they are going to try to say I'm being neglectful.* The social worker helped with our referral for Early Intervention but that was also a long process which required interviews, meetings, and evaluations to actually see if he qualified for help. As long as he met all their criteria he would be approved.

During the waiting period I kept doing the "at home" messaging and exercises. I knew how to do them because I learned from the parental support group, picked up some pointers from the internet, additionally, at that point I knew it would be a while before we actually got any help from anyone. My pain turned into my driving force to make sure I was everything our son needed. I was his therapist, I was his mother, I was his prayer warrior, I needed to stand in the gap for him, so as hurt as I was, I stood firm and I prayed and read my Bible. God gave me a scripture to read to Micah *"Then he said to me, 'Prophesy to these bones and say to them, Dry bones, hear the word of the Lord! This is what the Sovereign Lord says to these bones: I will make breath enter you, and you will come to life. I will attach tendons to you and make flesh come upon you and cover you with skin; I will put breath in you, and you will come to life. Then you will know that I am the Lord."* Ezekiel 37:4-5 NIV.

I started an Instagram page for Micah that documented all his progress. I was able to have a community of people through social media and spoke to other mothers going through the same situation. In the UK, India, even right here in the United States there were children suffering the same kind of injury. So many families were trying to navigate this new part of life without having much information to guide them. I was so surprised at how much this birth injury happens, but I had not heard anyone talk about it until it happened to them. While I was still unsatisfied with the level of medical attention Micah was receiving I continued to do my research and bought him toys that helped with range of motion and stretching. I continued to be all that I had to be for him. One day I was listening to a Kari Jobe song & Micah's arm jerked a little. No therapy from a licensed physical therapist. No surgery to heal his nerve damage. He finally moved on his own! Although the movement was small, in the grand scheme of things he had won a medal for reaching an incredible milestone in his 3 months of life so far.

I called Stephen and I cried, and we thanked God and posted the victory to his Instagram page. Micah continued to meet his developmental milestones. Some later than others but he has always been a trooper. He has always been the picture of perseverance and strength even as a baby. I've always heard that children were resilient and I began to understand that.

Micah continued physical therapy and we never limited him. Kids need to be able to explore their boundaries within the safety net of their parents and we learned that first hand with Micah. He taught me that life might hand you a really horrible deck of cards but that doesn't mean you're out of the game. We kept going no matter what. Micah never even knew he was handed a bad deck. Even now at seven years old he sees himself like any other happy, smart, energetic, running, jumping, climbing, sports playing little boy. God knew that this test would turn into an incredible testimony.

7
FIGHT!

Carly P. Bushelle

The doorbell rang, and I quickly scurried back upstairs, and into the room we shared. "I'll be back,"
she said, "don't come downstairs until I call you."
She left and closed the door behind her. They crammed the
room with two twin sized beds, a gargantuan hardwood
dresser with an enormous mirror, and a desk topped with a
black and white television set. I sat in that room and played
by myself until the curiosity that filled my mind got the best
of me. "Who is downstairs? What are they talking about
and why do I always have to sit here, in this room, by myself,
waiting for the coast to be declared safe enough for me to
make my presence known again? What's the big secret and
why?" Overcome by my inquisitiveness, I jerked open the
door, which always seemed to betray my trust in its ability
to remain silent whenever there were visitors. As I breached
its secure hold, I made my way to the top of the stairs and
shimmied down on my butt, one step at a time. About half

way down, someone noticed my feet and inquired about my identity, asking who I am and to whom I belong.

Before long, I made it to the bottom of the stairs. "Lauren, see what she wants."

"Hello," the guest of honor said, "what's your name?"

Before I could respond, she did. "Oh, her name is Carly; Lauren is just watching her until her mother gets home from work. She's an accountant, so you know, she works long hours. Carly, say hello to Ms. So and So."

I shyly said, "hello" before I was quickly whisked away; back upstairs and into the room by Lauren before the guest asked any more questions, or I shed more clarity on my seemingly mysterious existence. This scenario played out repeatedly; the story line remained the same; the only difference being the faces of the visitors inquiring. Over and over, this scene played until the once "first-time visitors" appearances became unannounced and far more frequent. Eventually, the observant visitor noticed the pattern, yet they said nothing. They stopped asking questions and just went along with the story.

I asked more questions as I became more cognizant. The questions become louder. The more I heard the story of my mother returning for me recounted to each unknown visitor, the louder they became. The days, the months, the years passed by. As I grew taller, I became more familiar with the room I shared with Lauren, the more questions I had. I sat there and thought to myself, *"where is my mother and when is she coming back for me?"* I stopped and looked in the mirror set atop that gargantuan dresser. As I stared at the reflection in the mirror, I wondered, *"do I look like her?"* I knew there had to be something in me that connected me to her beyond my questions about her. I plopped down on Lauren's bed and wondered about my mother. *"Does she think of me? Has she seen any recent pictures of me? What does her voice sound like?"* One day as I glanced at the mirror, I noticed it tucked tightly in the top corner between the frame and the reflective glass which provoked such strong questions. Every time I stood there, I stopped a bit longer than the time before, long enough to take in more of my features. This time, my glance made me take a second look and I saw it for the first time. It was the picture that stopped me dead in my tracks. It was a picture of Lauren. Her beautiful smile and her bright eyes called me back. She was draped in a cap and gown. That beautiful smile and those bright eyes softly sang a song of pride in her accomplishment of graduating. That song pulled me in and as I looked closer, I noticed a striking resemblance between that picture and my own reflection. It was in our eyes! Those bright, beady eyes looked just like mine, and though I couldn't make out all the words of the song they sang to me, that day, they made me feel even more connected to Lauren for reasons which at that time were unbeknownst to me. I don't remember when it happened or why but, one day I received the answer to the loudest question in my mind, *"who is my mother, where is she and when is she coming back for me?"* Everything became clear to me at that moment. My mother was never returning for me, because she never left me. She was always there! She was with me in that room. Day in and day out, when I noticed the undeniable resemblance and the unshakable connection I felt by looking at the picture of Lauren, it served as a confirmation of the truth that would eventually become too big, too real to hide. One day years down the line when my father heard me refer to her as Lauren, he inquired about why I was calling her by her first name and insisted that I call her "mommy." Although I would learn that Lauren was, in fact, my mother, the dynamics of my family situation took years for me to understand. So why was this a kept secret for so long? Growing up with my grandmother, she would always tell me the story of the day I was born. The shame and secrecy associated with my existence was because my mother was only 13 years old when she gave birth to me and 15 by the time my brother was born.

On Monday mornings, my mother would gather my brother and me and hurriedly take us over to the babysitter's house before rushing off to fulfill her duties as a student not yet out of high school. We wouldn't see her again until Friday evening, when she'd return to pick us up from the babysitter's house. Week in and week out, this routine continued for at least three years. Determined to make the best of the hand life dealt her, my mother left my brother and me in the babysitter's care, whom she trusted and to care for us in her absence while she balanced being a teenage mother and completing her middle and high school education.

Ms. Nelson's house became my second home. I spent more time there than I did at "home" with my family and though it should have been a place where I felt safe, it was quite the opposite. Instead, it became the first place I came to associate with many of my deep-rooted fears and feelings of vulnerability. It became the place where I first felt voiceless. It was the breeding ground for many of the choices I would make throughout my life that set me on a mission to self-destruct. Inside the four walls of that large blue house, set in the middle of a relatively quiet block, lay "secrets." These "secrets" informed my earliest memories of the development of my perception of myself as a sexual being.

Besides being a childcare facility, where parents left their most precious gifts, their innocent children, Ms. Nelson's home was a "safe place" for men with more "colorful lives" than others to carry out their devious acts. Slick and Kyle, two young men who were placed in Ms. Nelson's home as foster children, were often charged with the responsibility of monitoring us younger children. After watching soap operas and daytime game shows like, "The Price Is Right," once the "big kids" returned from school Ms. Nelson would leave us younger (preschool aged) children with them for them to entertain us while she retreated to her room to smoke her Marlboro cigarettes for what felt like hours at a time in another part of the house.

"Hey guys, today, we are going to play a new game. We are going to be in teams. Now, each of us put one foot in the circle." Excited, each of us put our feet into the circle. "Eenie, meanie, minnie, moe, catch a tiger by the toe, if it hollers, let it go, eenie, meanie, minnie, moe." Round and around the circle Kyle and Slick went, taking turns to pick who would be on their team. Finally, Kyle picked me. As the last person picked and the youngest girl in the bunch, I felt like I'd just earned a badge of honor. "Alright Rosebud (my nickname given by Ms. Nelson), come with me so I can explain how the game goes." Eagerly, I followed Kyle to the back of the house and into the bathroom. Once inside the bathroom, Kyle closed the door behind me, turned on the light, and locked the bathroom door behind us. Inside the bathroom, on the cold, hard, tiled floor, was a multi-colored fringed bath mat. Kyle doled out "instructions to the game" as he reached across the bathtub to grab a bottle filled with pearl colored liquid. He unbuttoned my pants and eased them down my thighs, past my knees, down to my ankles. "Lay down and be silent," he instructed me. "Part of this game is being able to keep a secret, this is our secret. Let me see if you can be quiet and help me keep our secret. If you can't then you can't be on my team," he added. As quietly as I could, I complied with his directions. "You're doing good. Now close your eyes, no peeking," he continued. While I laid there, I tried hard not to focus on the pain. I tried to block out how heavy his body felt on top of mine. The weight of his body, compounded by the darkness and immediate sense of guilt was enough to slowly suck the the life out of me until one day I completely disconnected myself from the little girl that laid there on the floor. Her innocence was snatched from her and she was now dead to me. "Keep your eyes closed and remember, you can't tell anybody our secret, plus if you do, they will not believe you, anyway. I'm almost done. Don't cry either, or they will ask you what's wrong and then call you a cry-baby," he warned. I obliged him and quickly wiped the tears from my eyes as I tried to ignore the unusual pain, coupled with the discomfort of the cold hard floor which was beneath me.

He stayed on top of me what felt like an eternity, jumping up frantically in response to the sound of the doorknob turning, followed by a knock on the door and a voice breaking the silence from the other side saying, "Hurry, what's taking y'all so long, we are ready to play the game."

"We're coming," he shot back.

Hurriedly, he grabbed a washcloth, ran it under cold water, and instructed me to wipe myself clean before he instructed me to put my underwear, pants, and shoes back on. Once I was dressed, he unlocked the door and let me out, reminding me again to be sure to keep "our secret." I did as I was told. Shortly after, he emerged from the bathroom and we proceeded to play the game as if nothing ever happened. From that day forward, it seemed like I always wound up on Kyle's team no matter what game we played, which led to more trips to the bathroom where he would force me to engage in sexual acts. As I got older and became more resistant to being on his team, his admonishments to keep the "secret" turned into threats that he would tell everyone what I did with him in the bathroom and warnings that I'd get in big trouble for, "being fresh" if Ms. Nelson or my mother found out. With each encounter, I became more and more numb. These types of encounters became "normalized" and I silently mourned the loss of my innocence there on that cold, hard bathroom floor. Feeling dirty and confused, ashamed and embarrassed, I held on to that "secret" for years. I don't recall ever actually articulating to anyone that I'd been raped and sexually abused several times by Kyle. I remained loyal to him by keeping my promise to not tell anyone. Outside, I maintained my appearance of innocence but inside, I carried guilt from those experiences for years. Stripped of my innocence, I blamed myself.

The faces of men who were in and out of the babysitter's house changed but I became more and more familiar with the feelings of fear and vulnerability while there. I recall seeing dark silhouettes of grown, faceless and nameless men who were passing through Ms. Nelson's house, entering the room where I slept in the middle of the night and the weight of their bodies pinning me down, my young impressionable mind focused only on pretending to be asleep until it was all over, looking forward to the morning light, from which they seemed to hide.

Sexual abuse was not the only type I was subjected to while in the babysitter's care. I can distinctly recall instances of sheer torture for the most minuscule infractions. Sitting at the dinner table, being forced to eat food that both smelled and tasted rancid. One evening, I literally became sick to my stomach. I tried to ask if I could excuse myself from the table, but Ms. Nelson ignored me and firmly reminded me that there was to be no talking at the dinner table. Not fully aware of my body's functionality (being no older than five years old), I tried with everything within me to control the bubbling sensation I felt filling my stomach from escaping, but I was unsuccessful. The sound and smell seemed to rumble through the kitchen, and Ms. Nelson's voice pierced through the awkward and smelly silence that lingered. "Who did that?" The other children at the table quickly exclaimed, "not me," "it wasn't me either," "it was Rosebud."

As quickly as they uttered my name, I felt the pain of her sharp, long fingernails digging into my ear as she yanked me up from the dinner table, barking expletives at me and dragging me towards the bathroom. "Get undressed, she commanded." Like always, I did as I was told. She ran the water in the bathtub for what I thought was going to be an early bath before going to bed. In my mind, though I hated the idea of having to go to bed earlier than the other children, I was happy to not have to continue eating the rancid food she'd prepared. Soon enough she filled the tub with water and instructed me to come closer to the tub. Ms. Nelson was seated on a stool near the tub. As I got closer and prepared to climb into the tub, I felt the sharp pains I'd experienced moments earlier at the dinner table, except this time the pain was from Ms. Nelson's nails digging into both sides of my neck. Before I knew it, my head was being thrust forward into the tub that was now filled with water. I struggled to make sense of what was happening. I could hardly talk or cry as Ms. Nelson held my head submerged in the water for what felt like several minutes. Enraged, after a while she let me go and reprimanded me for not excusing myself from the table. Afterwards, she bathed me and ordered me to bed. That was the first instance I can associate with the deathly fear of drowning that I'd developed over the years.

Somewhere around the time that I was 7 or 8 years old, my father re-entered my life. Our routine for spending the nights at Ms. Nelson's house continued, though on a somewhat sporadic basis. One Friday night, I recall that my mother took a lot longer than usual to pick us up. Eventually, the doorbell rang, just as I was drifting off to sleep. Eyes heavy and tired from crying; fearful that perhaps she wasn't coming back for us. It was my mother. She hurriedly rushed us out of the house and into a cab that was waiting for us. Inside the cab was my father. The cab took an unfamiliar route, and I realized we weren't going "home." That night, my father sat my brother and I down and explained that we weren't going back to my grandmother's house. He also explained that we were finally going to be a "happy family," that my grandmother tried to keep him away from us because she didn't want us to be a family and that she disliked him. He also established the rule that from that day forward, we were never to ask about or mention our aunts or our grandmother again. In fact, we could forget that they ever existed because we would never see them again. It was a lot for me to take in at the moment. I was happy to be a part of a "family" but the thought of never seeing my grandmother and aunts again saddened me. I was excited to have a room to call my own, though I shared it with my brother, it was big and spacious but somehow it didn't take away the feeling that we were being isolated from the world, I guess because that's exactly what was happening. I wouldn't see or hear from my mother's side of the family for several years.

Soon after we moved, both my brother and I became the targets of my father's anger. As the days and nights progressed, my father's anger towards me increased and I could sense the great level of disdain that he felt towards me. It soon felt like the only reason I existed was for him to torture me. He hated me! It seemed like I could do nothing right in his eyes, and he'd never accept or truly love me the way I imagined a father should.

"Carly, bring me some water," he'd shout from his room, "and hurry up!"

I'd come rushing down the stairs from my bedroom which was in the attic, trying to move as quickly as I could to fulfill his demands before the barrage of verbal insults ensued. "Here's your water daddy."

He'd take a sip. "It's not cold enough. Did you spit in it? Take it back and get me some more."

I'd rush to the kitchen and let the water run a little longer than the first time, hoping it reached a satisfactory temperature. "Here you go daddy."

He'd snatch the glass out of my hand and I'd turn to walk away. "Sit down, where are you going, did I tell you to move?"

"No daddy," I'd reply.

"Fix your face, look at you, you look miserable like your aunt Dana, I hope you don't turn out to be a whore like her, get out of here, looking at you is making me sick."

Day after day, the verbal assaults kept coming. Eventually, my father stopped calling me Carly and began calling me "Ugmug." He explained it was because my face was "so ugly" and he encouraged my brother to address me the same way. Over time, I developed thick skin and determined within myself that I would not let him break me but with each passing day, the fallacy of the adage, "Sticks and stones may break my bones but words will never hurt me" became more clear. That was the farthest thing from the truth. My father's words cut me to the core, so much so that I wondered if it even mattered to him if I lived or died. At age ten, I saw no future for myself if it meant that the rest of my life would be this way. I wished I were dead!

It was not long before my father changed his tactics and found novel ways to terrorize me. There were many nights when, in the middle of the night, I'd jump up out of my sleep shivering, or writhing in pain and crying. My father would make his way into the kitchen, where he would inspect the condition of the kitchen I had the duty of cleaning. It was my responsibility to make sure I cleaned the space to his liking. The slightest spot on a dish or between the prongs of a fork. The smallest crumb left unswept was enough reason for him to beat me. Often, he'd startle me out of my sleep by dousing me with frigid cold water, followed by powerful whacks across my buttocks, back and legs with a hard plastic cutting board from the kitchen, or an extension cord. As he'd unleash his fury, he'd yell, curse and demand that besides having to get up immediately to right the wrong I'd committed, I'd have to sleep standing up for the rest of the night. Sometimes, this punishment would include me standing with both arms fully extended and one leg up. If, for any reason, I dropped my arms, or he caught me with my foot touching the floor, I'd be beaten again, but this time with a leather work belt – my father was an construction worker. I'd be made to stand with my palms facing upward, balancing hardcover dictionaries or other heavy textbooks from school.

Of all the ways my father had punished me, the worst by far was when he'd make me stay home from school. Although my brother and I wore the same two outfits to school week in and week out and we were often teased and bullied because of it, school was the place I'd grown to see as my place of refuge. On days when I did not go to school, if not being forced to stand for hours on end holding my arms out, I'd be made to stay in the push-up position for hours. My father would often stack the dictionaries on my back to ensure that I maintained the proper posture. On some occasions, out of sheer fatigue from maintaining such a position for hours on end, it would become too much for me to handle, and I'd sneak and rest. While most times, I'd be able to hear if my father was coming into the living room and I'd quickly assume the position, I'd struggle to get the dictionaries back on top of me or I'd doze off to sleep. These instances were dead giveaways of me not complying with what he'd told me to do and would cause me to get beat and having to stay that way throughout the night or until he felt satisfied that I'd learned my lesson. For me, being in school meant that I would get to eat a full meal, at least for breakfast and lunch. When at home, there was always enough food for my father to eat like a king. While he'd enjoy meals of steak and potatoes, meals for my brother and I often comprised Peanut Butter and Jelly Sandwiches, Pot Pies and if it was a good day, then perhaps my brother and I would have hotdogs or canned spaghetti and meatballs. Most times while I'd eaten, it usually wasn't enough to satisfy my hunger.

Around the age of nine, I discovered my father had a drug addiction. His binges were a sign to me I'd have the liberty to eat and enjoy the novelties of childhood, at least for a few moments of fear. The drugs changed my father and in some ways, protected us from him. I learned early on that my father's drug binges would keep him out, in the streets for two to three days at a time, which essentially meant that for those 48-72 hours, I didn't have to live in fear of when the next beating or verbal onslaught would occur. In fact, when he returned home, it was quite the opposite for at least the next day or two. He was quiet. He expressed emotions.

He cried – a lot. He apologized for how he treated me, he promised to change, and he professed his love for me. These moments were short lived as they only lasted for as long as it took for the high to wear off completely. Before long, it was back to life as usual and I was walking on egg-shells around him. It got to where I guiltily wished he'd go out and get high just so we could have a few days without him terrorizing me. As dysfunctional as that may sound, it was my truth.

By the time I entered the sixth grade, my father took a fresh interest in me and suddenly, I seemed to be his favored child. He was suddenly "proud" of me and I could do very little wrong in his eyes. The complex we lived in had a sandbox with a swing set. While my mother was working to provide for the family, and I was being kept home from school, if my brother was home, my father would send him to play in the sandbox and explicitly instructed him to stay outside until he called for him. Once he could see my brother in the playground from our third-floor apartment window, my father would call me into his bedroom. Upon my entry, there I would find my father laying in bed with nothing more than his underwear and a "wife beater". My father would instruct me to lie down next to him. He'd begin by telling me how proud he was that I would graduate from sixth grade. He would encourage me to think about how I wanted to celebrate the event. After a few minutes of laying there talking, my father would encourage me to relax. He then pinned me down on the bed and sexually abused me. He would insist that there was nothing wrong with what he was doing because he was simply, "trying to teach me what not to let anyone else do to me." My father would explain to me I was not to share what he'd done with anyone else because it could get him in trouble because people would misunderstand it. Once he finished, he would instruct me to go take a shower. Once alone in the bathroom, I would cry because I hated what was happening and yet I didn't have the power to stop it. Like Kyle, my father took away from my sense of innocence and protection. He would tell me that if I said anything, no one would believe me and they would think that I was a liar or that I would ruin our family if I shared what I was experiencing. Once again, I swore myself to secrecy as I'd done with Kyle. Deep down, while I knew something was wrong with what was happening, the only person I saw as worthy of blame was me, because I allowed it to happen. Family outings always followed these incidents as a "treat" for me being on my "best behavior." My father would insist that we celebrate by having dinner at a neighborhood restaurant. These were the only times when I could choose anything I wanted to eat from the menu.

Around eleven years old, I sensed that my history of being sexually abused was something that was just a "normal" way of life for some. Surely, this must have been an experience that all girls must go through in their lives. Seeing myself as the common denominator in each of those situations stemming back to around four years of age, I wondered if there was something wrong with me. Perhaps something I said, something I did, something I was wearing must have communicated that I wanted these men and I wanted to give myself to them in that way. These thoughts that seemed to scream out in the corridors of my memory every time I replayed the various incidents in my mind haunted me. No matter how hard I tried to forget my experiences, I couldn't. What's worse was the fact that somewhere deep down inside of me, while I knew there was something wrong with these situations, there was a part of me that liked the way I felt knowing that these men "trusted" me with such "grown up secrets." They must have seen some type of value in me. I must have been special to them and I must have done a pretty good job satisfying whatever needs they had, because they kept coming back to me and they seemed happy. Those thoughts made me feel good. Those thoughts made me feel significant. Someone *saw* me, someone *needed* me. I had a place in this world and a clear role to fulfill in the lives of these men. No matter who equated my presence with shame, these men didn't! Those thoughts made me believe that perhaps my value and worthiness depended on how well I could satisfy the sexual needs of a man yet, in all of this, I remained confused. Why did I feel so horrible? Why did I feel so dirty after every encounter? Why was it that every time I looked in the mirror after each encounter, every time someone commented on how beautiful, how kind, how caring or intelligent I was, all I could hear or see were huge black letters that read, "WARNING: DAMAGED GOODS?"

Deeply conflicted by my thoughts and feelings, I resolved within myself that the best way for me to cope with the pain of repeatedly being violated sexually was to say nothing about it at all. As a result, early on, a seed was planted in my mind that the only way to not feel as though I was being violated sexually whenever I found myself in an uncomfortable situation was to not fight the feeling and just go with the flow. I was convinced that if I allowed myself to be okay with what was happening, then I had a level of control over the situation because I was making a choice to engage, or so I thought. It never dawned on me that I had the right to say, "no" because my power to do so was stripped away from me the very first time I was sexually abused on that cold bathroom floor of the babysitter's house before I could even spell the word NO.

Having accepted Christ as my personal savior at fourteen years old was the best decision I could have ever made; however, that decision came with great internal struggle and a fight which took several years for me to overcome. As I matured in Christ, I learned that one of the foundational elements of living victoriously as a Christian is understanding and accepting one's identity in Christ. Because of the years

I spent as "the family secret" and the repeated sexual abuse, I found it difficult to accept that I belonged in the family of God. I struggled to believe that my life had a purpose, and that there was a reason for my existence. I also struggled to believe that God's love for me was unconditional and irrevocable. I constantly needed affirmation and approval from others to confirm my legitimacy as an individual of significance and value. Sitting in rooms full of people, I felt alone. Surrounded by people who embraced me, I found it challenging to settle in and become comfortable because I lived with the belief that if my family could treat me as if I were insignificant, then there was no reason for anyone else to act otherwise. I found it difficult to let my guard down and the older I got, the greater this need for a place to "belong" and a sense of acceptance grew. To meet this need, I found myself "looking for love in all the wrong places and all the wrong faces." This often resulted in me living in a constant state of insecurity and engaged in a cycle of toxic relationships, which confirmed the faulty belief that I was insignificant and fed my feelings of shame. As a Christian I felt unworthy. I was living a double life. I knew what the Word of God had to say about fornication and sexual sin, yet I couldn't find my way to freedom from its grips. I became convinced that this yoke of bondage would always be a part of my life. I found it difficult to be honest about my struggles in this area for fear of judgment because after all... *"I should have been past this by now. I know the Word. All it takes is prayer and a mind to do right.*" Those statements offered as words of wisdom and guidance from church leaders in whom I confided were instead used as weapons by the enemy to make me feel suffocated by guilt, shame, judgment and hopelessness. I struggled silently all while serving in the church. I'd fallen into a lifestyle of sexual promiscuity and found myself stuck in a cycle of sexual sin repeatedly. Though I wished it were that easy, the fact remained it wasn't. I always felt convicted about my actions, yet most of the time I could not muster up the courage to confess or ask for help, prayer or anything of the sort for fear of being judged and rejected or isolated. As a result, I would silently endure heartbreak after heartbreak and disappointment after disappointment that came along with each failed and often clandestine relationship.

I thought this cycle was over when I met and married the man who, on paper, met my laundry list of requirements for a potential spouse. Having meticulously checked off each criterion on my list, I entered what some would call a "whirlwind relationship". We began dating and married in a matter of ten months. A year into our relationship and two months after marrying, I discovered I was pregnant with twins. I was scared, but elated. Finally, the "story book ending" to my life was unfolding. I had a husband. I was going to have two children who I could call my family. What more could I ask for? Surely the roles of wife and mother were enough to silence the chattering teeth of the proverbial skeletons I'd so neatly tucked into the closets of my life. Boy, was I wrong!

My breaking point in this cycle of "love gone wrong" came as a failed marriage. After a little over two years, my happily ever after came to an earth shattering end. The failure of my marriage I thought, could be attributed to several things including my choice to ignore several "red flags" and my failure to listen to the few trusted individuals in my life who honestly shared their concerns about the quick pace of my relationship, one of the greatest contributors on my part was my false sense of security built upon false or misplaced expectations. I entered the marriage thinking that someone was going to love me unconditionally and stay by my side as we'd vowed, "til death had finally found me do us part." My identity became wrapped up in being his "wife" and the twins "mother" and I lost sight of God and struggled to hear His voice as I attempted to handle the pressures of being a wife and mother. For my eagerness to take on these roles I expected from him: validation, support and affirmation. I expected undying love, patience, understanding and an unwavering commitment. Unbeknownst to me, I was expecting my husband to be the healer to everywhere I hurt. I expected him to fill the god-sized voids in my heart. I expected him to remind me of my significance and to show me my worth daily through his words and his actions. I was looking for a level of love that only God himself could give, yet I didn't realize until he pulled the rug from under me and had me served with divorce papers, a year and a half into our marriage.

I'd built my hopes and dreams for a beautiful and bright future on a very faulty foundation that was crumbling before my very eyes. I was thoroughly devastated and completely embarrassed every time I stepped foot inside my home church. I dreaded responding to altar calls given during church because he proposed at the altar. The place that once held memories of times I felt closest to God had now become the place I wanted to avoid the most because it reminded me of the greatest failure of my life. The feelings of shame only grew, and I felt even more isolated than I'd ever felt before. I had to let God handle this, even though I couldn't understand why He'd allow things to happen the way they did. It was too much for me. I soon realized as time went on how necessary that part of my life's journey was.

The painful process of divorce and coming to terms with my failures in the public spotlight of the church, forced me to come to terms with some of the life choices I made. I finally decided to be honest with myself and God about the reasons which fueled the many years of self-sabotaging decisions I made. Having come to the point in life when what was supposed to be a lifelong relationship came to an abrupt and world-shattering end, I faced my biggest fear. I finally had to confront Satan's false accusations that I was alone, unloved, and unlovable. I had to answer his false charges that I was a mistake, insignificant and worthless. I had to answer every one of his claims as I stood face to face with the fears that held me in their grip for as long as I could remember.

Going through the process of divorce forced me to rely totally on God to carry me through that season of my life. All I had to stand on was God's Word and faith that if He brought me *to* this point, then certainly He would bring me *through* it. It was through that experience that I came to know God more intimately as "I Am, that I Am." I felt like I was being stripped naked for the world to see me, and I was completely vulnerable. I had nothing and no one else to hide behind. The title of "wife" was stripped away from me and although during this time I was active in church as a leader, I didn't feel worthy of that title either. I felt like a complete failure and I was convinced that's what others thought of me as well. Navigating that process, though surrounded by people I know loved me, was a very lonely and dark experience and while people may have wanted to be there and empathize with me, they couldn't. While some said they would be there for me, in reality they weren't. It was during that season that I learned that my identity wasn't to be wrapped up in what any other human being called me or what role I played in the lives of anyone else or vice versa. I had to learn that while God can use others to show His love towards me through my interpersonal relationships with them, I should never predicate my significance and legitimacy as an object of His affection and my identity as His beloved daughter upon those relationships. The failure of other relationships should never be able to cause me to question or doubt the faithfulness of God and His love and purpose for me, nor should it cause me to question who I am in Him.

8
HEAVEN FOR 17 DAYS

Shanay Howard

The day I found out I was pregnant was an amazing day. My husband (Isaac-Ike) and I were filled with excitement! We couldn't wait to tell our family and everyone! This was our gift from the Lord, birthed out of the marriage He gave us. Isaac and I were ready for this! In our heads, this was the perfect time to have a baby. We had been married for three years and it was time to add to the party!

The pregnancy went very well! Every appointment, examination, check-up and test I had came back with good reports. Nothing was wrong, everything was going great! I felt good. I continued to coach my basketball teams and we even won a championship! While carrying my beautiful daughter I even continued to work full time and maintained my daily schedule. The closer we got to the due date, the more excited we became. Every kick I felt and every sonogram I saw, I fell in love more and more.

I even had two baby showers! I live in VA, but was born and raised in NY. I had my first shower in Northern VA and it was just beautiful; all my friends came and gave gifts to shower Heaven. They too were excited. Then one weekend later we headed to NY, to have another shower given by my family and friends. Again, everyone was excited and ready to meet my baby girl – Heaven Renee. Heaven was blessed way before she entered the earth.

The due date came and Heaven stayed in her cocoon. This was to be expected since it was my first pregnancy. This was normal according to the doctors and all the documentation that I read. Plus I heard many stories about babies coming either two weeks early or two weeks past their due date. There was no cause for concern, so I went on with my daily activities and waited in anticipation to meet my beautiful baby girl. Then two days later around 10pm, I felt it was time! My husband and I were watching television and I said, "Babe, I think its time to go." He jumped up, grabbed the car keys and off we headed to the hospital.

When we got to the hospital we were admitted and prepped. I wasn't fully dilated but the doctor wanted to keep me and said the baby would be arriving early the next morning. This was it! I was ready! It was GO time!

FAST FORWARD. Labor started. I didn't know how it would go but it all seemed to be going very well. The doctor and nurses repeatedly came in and out of the room to check my and the baby's vitals to make sure all was well. Suddenly around 4 A.M., the doctor said that it was time to push. The baby was coming, and I was ready! I pushed, then she said, "Stop!" Then she said, "Push!" again, then another, "Stop!" This went on for some time until a shift in the atmosphere happened. Something seemed wrong! I could tell by the doctor's face. I could tell by the number of nurses and other people who started to come into the delivery room. I asked what was happening, and one person answered, "We gotta get the baby out you gotta push." I said, "I am pushing," while the tears began to run down my face. I was scared. I did not know what was happening and everything seemed intense. They put an oxygen mask on me and told me I had to calm down. There was so much going on and all I could do was pray! I didn't have many words. I only had Jesus! I just began to say His Name over and over again, "Jesus, Jesus, Jesus!"

The nurses and doctors were trying to calm me down but as I looked over to my right and saw my baby being brought back to life the emotions racing through my psyche were out of control. I was scared! I was confused! Worry and concern swelled in my belly! I did not know what to think, how to feel, as I was really clueless as to what could have happened in such a short space of time. I looked at my husband and he tried to look calm but I knew something was not right. There were too many people in the room. The baby came out, they placed her on me for a second then she was taken. They kept saying, "Shanay it is ok, calm down. Shanay, it is ok just calm down." My heart rate escalated, my blood pressure was high, and they were anxious about my overall well being. However, all I could think of was my baby.

They brought her back to me, just in time to ship her to the NICU. I barely saw her. It was so quick. What happened? This was not what I planned! This was not how I imagined it was going to be. Just a few hours prior, I was so excited as we headed to the hospital. Couldn't wait to see her and hold her in my arms. All that changed in a blink of an eye. *"Why God, why?"*

Hours later I was told she needed to be sent by medivac to a Specialist Hospital in DC. This was more serious than expected.

I just sat in the hospital bed shaking my head and thinking: *"This isn't what I planned. This is not what I thought would ever happen! This is not what they show in the movies of a healthy birth. Why is this happening?"*

FAST FORWARD.

The Specialist Hospital.

On the second day after giving birth, I woke up in a chair, that would be my bed in The Specialist Hospital. The sounds of beeps got my full attention. Beep.. beep.. beep as my slumber was disturbed. "How did I get here? Why did this happen to me? Why me?" As tears ran down my face, I asked God, "Why?" and so many other questions. I looked over at the place where my baby laid. She had tubes in her nose, wires connected to her chest, a cuff on her ankle and a code (cold) blanket under her head. They told me they were cooling her brain. Unfamiliar medical terms and procedures were passed on to me earlier that day, but I just couldn't fathom what it all meant – until I saw her. I sat up in the chair and cried with my head buried in my hands. I sobbed and sobbed. I got down on the floor. On my knees I cried some more and I tried to pray. All that came out when I began was a litany of questions:

"God, why?"
"Do you see her?"
"She is helpless!"
"How can You help her?"
"How can I help her?"
"Did I do this?"

"Lord, please help her. Lord please help me. Lord please do something! I can't bear to see her like this." Never did I imagine my baby would be on a table fighting for her life. I never even knew people went through things of this magnitude.

I finally got up off my knees and couldn't go back to sleep. I just stared at my baby. She was beautiful even with all those tubes. Her head was full of hair. I took a moment and thought, *"Wow God, she came from me?"*

No one was really telling me much. I watched as nurses came in and out like clockwork every hour to check and read the machines. I saw numbers and heard beeps and didn't know what any of them meant. It seemed as though the nurses were instructed not to give us too much information.

The next day came and in walked the doctors. They asked to meet with my husband and me. I said ok. I was curious and anxious wanting to know what was going on and how soon my baby would be getting out of there. I wanted to know when they would wake her up so I could see her eyes. We walked into a room where five people greeted us – all doctors and specialists. They began to talk and said that Heaven was not responding to the treatment but they would continue to watch until the whole process went through. They began to tell me this was a rare occurrence and they could not determine the cause of it yet. They only knew that the umbilical cord had wrapped itself around her neck upon delivery. I knew enough to know that would cause Asphyxia, but not much more. However, her situation appeared a little more serious than that.

Days passed and she was no longer cooling. During the days Ike and I prayed and we prayed hard that Heaven would make a miraculous turn around in health. Each day during that time, doctors came by and said nothing changed. We were still hopeful. We had faith. Then the cooling was done. And her eyes did not open. She was breathing but she wasn't moving much. What's going on?? I was so confused. We prayed. Usually, in the past, that's all I needed to do. I wasn't eating. So, technically I was fasting. I couldn't eat. My body was hurting. My heart ached. It had been four days and I hadn't been home since giving birth – I just couldn't leave her. I told myself I wasn't leaving until she did.

It was time for another doctors' meeting. Same five people met with us, but this time they had brain scans for us to view. I didn't know what they meant, I didn't even know what to look for. They started to speak and all I remember from that conversation was that Heaven's brain cells were dying and parts of her brain were not functioning as they should. Basically, it was not looking good. I didn't retain much after that. I zoned out! How was this happening? The meeting ended and I remember sitting in the room until all the doctors left. It was just Isaac and me. I bursted into tears, and said, "God has to do something! I know He can do it! He just has to do something." Ike held me close and said, "We have to trust God. I know what the doctors said, but we just have to trust God."

For the next 13 days, that's all we did! We trusted God! Our families trusted God. Our church families trusted God with and for us. We had a strong prayer support. The hospital and doctors had given their reports – we knew they didn't think Heaven would make it another day! Every day, during the next 13 days she showed us something. They said she wouldn't react but one day when we pulled her leg, she snatched it back.. They said she wouldn't breath on her own – she did that on day 16. God was performing miracles in the midst of our storm and showing us that even though it didn't look promising, He was there.

Ike and I spent those days in the hospital, praying with other couples we met who became neighbors to Heaven with their children. They also received negative news at times, so we prayed with them. In our 16 days there we met four couples and their babies. God was showing us that this journey was bigger than Heaven, Isaac and me.

It was the 16th day in the hospital and Isaac and I were praying. God encouraged us with these words "No matter the outcome, I, The Lord will be with you." We told the doctors, it was time for Heaven to be off the tubes and that she would breathe on her own when they did it. It was not easy for them to do it and they thought we were crazy, but they did it and she breathed.

SHE BREATHED ON HER OWN. I held my baby for the first time in16 days with no tubes. In my arms she breathed. I smiled and tears fell. God had performed a miracle right before our eyes. The doctors told us, if we removed the tubes she wouldn't last two minutes. Heaven breathed without tubes and on her own for the next 15 hours but, on May 5th 2018, she took her final breath in my arms. My beautiful baby girl was ushered into the arms of our Loving Lord with me singing praises to the King of Kings and the Lord of Lords. She peacefully entered through God's Heavenly gates leaving behind all the cares of this earth. I thought I would be broken but, instead I was so amazed at how peaceful and beautiful the experience was. My baby had received her ultimate healing and that is what we prayed for.

Of course, I would have loved to have had my baby girl here with us, but, I'm certain, she would have been hindered in some capacity according to all the reports we received. God gave her full healing! From 4/18/18 to 5/5/18 my baby girl lived and defied the odds of the doctors. God gave Isaac and me time to not only become closer but, He strengthened our faith in Him.

Sometimes things don't turn out the way we want them to, or plan for them to happen; but God is always there. God was with us the entire time and we experienced Him first hand.

Yes, I miss my daughter a great deal. I think of her every day, but the Lord has restored my soul and heart. He has given me the strength to live daily and to live for her. The doctors said we wouldn't get two days and we got 17 days. I am forever grateful. for each day I got to spend with my daughter and God reminds me daily this isn't the end of my story.

I truly learned God's sovereignty in this experience. I had to ask myself, *"did I trust Him?"* It was clear cut: Either I believed God's Word, or I didn't. All I can say is I still believe God! He took my pain and turned it into faith. I learned to trust God past my circumstances and what I could see.

I filled a storage unit with all Heaven's gifts and clothes. When I closed the gate, God said, "This is not the end!" And it wasn't the end. The Lord blessed me with another child. Several months after the passing of Heaven, I shockingly found out I was pregnant. I couldn't believe it because I just didn't know how it happened. But then, I remembered God is a promise keeper! This was His "promise baby" to me, my rainbow after the storm and He was reminding me He heard all my cries. Ciela Joy Howard was born 3/3/2019, just a little over 10 months after Heaven was born. This was a major experience. I literally relived every bit of Heaven's pregnancy all over again! I had to walk through my trauma while still being pregnant with my gift and promise.

This was no easy task and I had to intentionally remind myself that God would complete the work He started in me *again* with this birth. I even had to walk through this *again* with my OBGYN. She too, experienced trauma from the first birth and loss but, we knew this pregnancy would be different. Of course, the hospital labeled me a high risk patient. I had way more visits than I did with Heaven, and all my visits included a specialist. Two things puzzled them. Firstly, the loss of Heaven and how that happened from a full term, healthy pregnancy. Secondly, I was sitting in front of them, months later, pregnant with another child, not completely broken! I was a walking testimony and I knew this was part of my ministry in this season for all who came in contact with me. I knew people would come to love the Lord because of my story and that's just what happened. The look on each doctor's face every time they met me for the first time, they would glance down at my chart, and then look at me again as if to say, "Wow, how is she here? Why is she here?" I knew it was for a greater purpose.

The doctors told me that I had a choice to have what they called a selective C-section with Ciela because of what happened with Heaven. Initially, I went with it. I didn't want to wait like I did before and I wanted to see my baby delivered as early as possible. God had a different plan! He knew my heart and that I needed to go through Ciela's birth the same way I did Heaven's to show me that I could do it and He was with me. So on March 3rd early in the morning, I woke up from my sleep with contractions. I knew the baby would come that day. I told my husband to get ready and we headed to the hospital. By the time we arrived, I was 7 centimeters dilated and began to get prepped for delivery. Ciela was on her way and I had a lot of mixed emotions. Everything was happening so fast, and then BAM! It hit me like a ton of bricks. Déjà vu. You know that, "I've been here before" feeling! But for me it really did happen! And my mind started to race, and I had to keep saying, "I will get through this, God is with me! This will be different than Heaven! She will live and not die!" With tears streaming down my face, I looked over to my husband who was holding my hand in the exact position he was with Heaven. I didn't say a word, I just looked at him and he knew my thoughts! It was so intense! He bent down to the side of my face and whispered in my ear, "You can do this!" It wasn't a sermon, it wasn't some big words, but it was just what I needed to hear. I had to fight every imaginable thought racing through my mind and then it happened... the last push! Ciela Joy was here! She came out screaming and I broke down... I mean tears, hyperventilating tears of joy! I waited almost two years to hear that sound. That sound I didn't get to hear with Heaven. I got to hold my baby and look into her eyes immediately, another thing I did not experience with Heaven. I was overwhelmed. My heart rate went all the way up and the doctors had to calm me down. The emotions took over my body; I was so thankful! It was all worth it! She was here!

I eventually calmed down. They cleaned up the baby and my readings normalized. I laid back and looked up and couldn't help but give God praise! I was alive, Ciela was alive! I remember saying to Heaven, "Your sis is here because of you!" When I looked down at Ciela, in my arms, the uncanny resemblance to Heaven was breathtaking but I know it was God once again reminding me of His promise. The process of Heaven's birth to her death to Ciela's birth was all one big testimony!

Today Ciela is 2 years old and thriving daily! We named her after her sister Heaven and Ciela Joy means "Heaven's delight." We will tell her when she is older the meaning of her name and the story of her older sister. Heaven's legacy will forever live on! What I went through was something

I thought would break me, but it only made me stronger and more in love with Jesus! I trust Him even more and know that His promises and His plans for me are all for good! I would encourage anyone reading this, to remember no matter what, God always wants to work things out, for your good.

9
WHO AM I?

Pauline Hunter

*"Not that I have already obtained all this, or have already been
made perfect, but I press on to take hold of that for which
Christ Jesus took hold of me. Brothers, I do not consider myself
yet to have taken hold of it. But, one thing I do; Forgetting what
is behind and straining toward what is ahead. I press on toward
the goal to win the prize for which God has called the
heavenward in Christ Jesus."*
Philippians 3:12-14, NIV

How many promises has God made to some of us,
that we question and wonder if they are true or if
they would ever come to pass? How many times
have we wondered if we really heard from God or we con-
jured it up because that is something we would desperately like to see happen? God made a promise to Sarah and
Abraham about having a son and it took what seemed like
eternity for the promise to be fulfilled. *"Then the word of the*

LORD came to him: 'This man will not be your heir, but a son coming from your own body will be your heir.'" Genesis 15:4 NIV

More than twenty years ago the Lord used one of his serv-ants to speak into my life telling me that my latter years would be greater than my former. *"Though your beginning was small, Yet your latter end would increase abundantly."* Job 8:7. Through my tunnel vision, I saw myself having a big house for my children, money in the bank and a nice car. That was me seeing my better years in material things. *"For the vision is yet for an appointed time, but at the end it shall speak, and not lie: though it tarry, wait for it; because it will surely come, it will not tarry."* Habakkuk 2:3, KJV. In other words, I was seeing it from a very small lens; putting a limit on God without rec-ognizing that He doesn't do things the way we humans do. How many of us have doubted that God is able to do what He says He would do in our lives because of past mistakes we have made or the family we were born in? Could it be that we feel inadequate because of where we live or a lack of education? Well, I trust after you read this snippet of an event that happened in my childhood, you will realize that, *"God is no respecter of person and will do what He says He will do because He's not a man and He cannot lie".* Numbers 23:19, NIV.

Let me introduce to you Pauline Angela Burns; I was born to two people who were not married. Some would say I was an illegitimate, but I'm so grateful to God that He doesn't see us as illegitimate according to Genesis 1:27 NKJV *"So God created man in His own image; in the image of God He created him; male and female He created them"*. At the time of my birth, my father, being older than my mother and she being unemployed, weren't living together and so I was left to be raised by my grandmother (who is now in heaven). I am reminded of the verse in Jeremiah 1:5a that alludes to the fact that God knew us before we were formed in our mother's womb. When God has a plan for your life, nothing in this world can stop or hinder the plans that God has for your life.

"For I know the plans I have for you, declares the LORD, plans to prosper you and not to harm you, plans to give you hope and a future." Jeremiah 29:11, NIV. God knew where He wanted me in this stage of my life and as a result, I had to be raised by my grandmother who would have raised me in the things of the Lord.

As the years went by, the time came for me to go to school and my grandmother sent my youngest aunt, who was living with us at that time, to register me for school. At the time I was born, and living in Jamaica,WI, you did not need to prove the date of birth or residency of a child in order to go to school. That is why my grandmother just wrote my name on a piece of paper and gave it to my aunt to take to school and register me. I was registered as "Grace Bourne", and I went through school for the first seven years of my educational life as Grace Bourne, only to discover that the name under which I was registered was not my correct name. I was teased constantly in school because of my name and after enduring all that abuse I found out it was for naught. According to society norms, I was "skinny" or as they would say in Jamaica, "mahga". The kids would tease me by saying that I was too ugly and as a result my father (the one they assigned to me, Mr. Lightbourne, who was a politician at the time), disowned me and so my mother dropped the "Light" and named me "Bourne". Of course, that wasn't the only form of abuse or bullying I experienced at their hands, but I will leave that for my book.

As I grew up, my grandmother used terms of endearment interchangeably by calling me either "Gracie" or "Angela" and I would answer to either of them until the day of reckoning came. It was time for me to register for what was then referred to as the "Common Entrance Exam", an Island-wide exam. This is the exam that would allow me to enter high school. In Jamaica, children could start high school as young as eleven and twelve years old and so when it came time for me to take the exam, my teacher had some work to do in registering us to take the exam. As she was going through the process and calling the students one by one for the needed information. When she got to my name, "Grace Bourne," I blurted out that that was not my name. Needless to say, that was a big shock to her. She called me to her desk, and

I told her that my name was Angela Burns. Evidently she would need proof and proceeded to tell me that I needed to bring in my "age paper" (birth certificate). Isn't it great that in God there is no confusion with our names? God knows what our names would be before we were born. He even knew who our parents would be which leads me to understand that none of us are mistakes. *"I praise you because I am fearfully and wonderfully made; your works are wonderful; I know that full well. My frame was not hidden from you when I was made in the secret place. When I was woven together in the depths of the earth."* Psalm 139:4-5 NIV. The world may treat us like mistakes, but there are no mistakes in God. He took His time when He created us and was deliberate in positioning us with the family in which we were born for His Glory. There are many examples in the scriptures where names were changed for the glory of God.

I went home and told my grandmother that my teacher wanted my "age paper". My grandmother gave it to me with a stern warning not to lose it. I took my birth certificate into school and gave it to my teacher. It was at that time, I realized that I was not legally registered as "Grace Bourne," but instead was registered as "Pauline Angela Burns." By the way, did I mention that not only was I not registered correctly for school, but even my birth certificate had the wrong birth month which had to be corrected when my dad tried getting a passport for me?

Needless to say, "Pauline Angela Burns" was something new to me. But as a child, when you have been called a name for so long, you are not worried about walking in a new name. Ask Jacob about having a new name; as God was all in his future. Even though his name means trickster, when God got through with him, he was no longer a trickster, but the person God intended him to be. *"The man asked him, 'What is your name?' 'Jacob,' he answered. Then the man said, 'Your name will no longer be Jacob, but Israel, because you have struggled with God and with men and have overcome.'"* Genesis 32:27-28 NIV.

It doesn't matter what you are called; God knows your name and has already mapped out the plan for your life. Yes, there are times when we might stray off path or have to take the long road to get there, but we will definitely come back to where we are supposed to be in order to have God's purpose fulfilled in our lives.

Fast forward ten years later, "Gracie" and her young twenty year old self are now living in a new country. Although she came to this new country as Pauline Angela Burns, Gracie didn't stay in Jamaica, she also came to America. In man's eyes, Gracie was not good for anything, she was just like her mother. Man's perception of you is one thing, but God already knows who you are and what you're supposed to be and therefore, no matter what is said about you, you must remember who God says you are.

So here I am in America with hopes that I would be able to go to school and do something with my life. But hold on a minute – not so – because I was too old for high school and there was no money for me to go to college so, the only choice I had then, was to go get a job. But, who was going to hire an individual with only a beginning high school education and no skills? My options were very slim, except maybe getting a job doing either domestic or childcare work, none of which I was interested in. (By the way, let me be clear that I have nothing against those jobs, but it was not what I wanted for myself.) There was one of three careers that I wanted to accomplish in life: teacher, pediatric nursing or family court lawyer. God gives each of us special gifts and it is up to us to develop those gifts that He has endowed us with. Remember now, we're talking about Gracie who is not going to do anything with her life; she's going to be "just like her mother." My fate was already sealed with negativity. But I'm reminded of Isaiah 54:17 which clearly states, *"No weapon formed against you shall prosper, and every tongue which rises against you in judgment you shall condemn. This is the heritage of the servants of the Lord, and their righteousness from Me."* Man's opinion of you doesn't matter; it is who God says you are that really matters. God says, I'm the head and not the tail and I'm blessed going out and coming in; God says, I'm fearfully and wonderfully made in the image and likeness of God. God further says that I am an heir to the seed of Abraham. This is what God says about me. Gracie lived for some years after, until Pauline decided it was time to step out of her shadow and walk instead into the true identity of Pauline Angela Burns.

As I was writing and doing some further research, I began accepting that the name Gracie wasn't totally bad after all. Looking back and realizing that if I remove the "i" from Gracie I would have the word "Grace" which is God's un-merited favor over my life. Even though the name appears to have a negative connotation in my upbringing, I now see through a different lens that it was definitely God's Grace that brought me to where I am today. And then looking at my given name Pauline, I could take away the "ine" and end up with the name Paul who was a mighty apostle of Jesus Christ. He suffered many things for the Gospel's sake; he had a thorn in his flesh and he prayed that the Lord would remove, but God did not remove it. Instead, the Lord told him in Acts 12:9a, *"My grace is sufficient for you, for my power is made perfect in weakness"*. Finally, regarding the name Angela, I will do a little play on words here. You see, I could remove the "a" from Angela and end up with the word "Angel."

In the Jamaican Patois there's a saying that says, "wat is fi you, can't be unfi you," meaning – **what is for you is for you.** God knows my name, He knew what I would become and He has fulfilled His promise of blessing me.

10
THE OTHER MAN

Elaina Monrae

Where do I start? There is so much to tell, so much to share. I guess it's always best to start at the beginning. I was 16 years old when I met my ex-husband at a church picnic. He was two years older than I was – I was in love. Being that young I knew so little about life and the direction in which I was headed. We didn't start dating until I was 17 and things were great. Here I was enjoying my first boyfriend, doing well in school, even got my first job; I was happy. Little did I know what the enemy had in store for me.

I knew about God. I knew He was around. I knew that He loved me because He had shown His love to me many times before. I just did not know Him for myself. He was the one my grandmother and her sisters would often talk about when they got together. They spoke of this God who loved all the little children. This was the God my grandfather preached about on Easter Sunday. He preached about a God who laid His life down for you and for me. I personally neither knew Him, nor did I have plans to get to know Him, but He knew me. He loved me and gave His life for me, although I was oblivious to His presence.

I was raised by a single mother who did the best she could in raising me, my sister and my brother. My father was around, but he remarried when I was a little girl. My stepmother also had a daughter around my age, so I was thankful for that. I always told myself, if I ever got married, divorce was not an option, because of the struggles I saw my mom endure. When I married my ex-husband, in my mind, it was for life, that is, till death do us part. I did not know he would try to take it literally. He was a talented, church going young man who was blessed with many gifts, such as singing, acting, dancing, and drawing. He was a superb artist, and he loved to play the guitar. To me, you named it and he could do it. I guess that is why most people he met either loved him or hated him.

His grandfather was a well-known Bishop of several churches on the west coast. The First Lady, affectionately known to the kids as "Auntie Millie," was always smiling. They had one boy and three girls who were equally talented in their own way. My mother-in-law was an Apostle and her family was blessed with gifts of prophecy, singing, and preaching.

Together, the families were phenomenal and the musical gifts were "off the chart." All those giftings were poured into my ex-husband and his siblings for the next generations to carry on. It's strange how the enemy can so easily distract us from our blessings if we are not set on a firm foundation.

When Ricardo asked me to marry him I was 22 and our daughter was about to be three years old. I was looking forward to a wonderful life together. Life was good. We had our ups and downs, but we just took them in stride as part of the challenges of being husband and wife. Example: for a while we struggled to keep an apartment so we became homeless and had to live with other family members until we could get back on our feet.

We both went to school to advance our options. I got my medical assistant license, and he became a teacher's assistant. We wanted to be independent, self-sufficient so that we could support our growing family. We worked hard. There were times that I had three jobs: two part time and one full time. He worked two full time jobs and we would alternate our work schedules while his mother would baby sit.

We planned on buying a house in a small suburb of Texas, and so I worked in the local hospital and he worked in the public school in our neighborhood. Our ultimate goal was to support ourselves and our family, however, things began to change. As we began to save up for our home, Auntie Millie became ill. As a result, family members began relocating to Murphy, Texas to assist her, knowing that she would eventually become a widow. She was all alone, living deep in the woods.

Ricardo became distracted, lost his focus, started listening to people outside of our marriage and taking their advice. Did I mention that his brother never liked me? I suspected it was because I was not a follower and would not allow people to take advantage of me or act a fool to entertain him or his sisters. However, his brother's ex-girlfriends were ready to play the fool at the drop of a hat. His sisters would let me know how much they did not like me and I would let him know how much I did not care whether they liked me or not! Ricardo started going out more, working less, and doing odd things like accusing me of seeing other people. I brushed it off and reassured him that I was not.

After a few months, Ricardo's mother and sister decided to go to Murphy, Texas to be with Pops, his father. That was when things really started to change. He began to lose focus on our plans to move to a suburb in Dallas, Texas, and focused more on an acting career. He would go to several acting studios at night and not return until early the next morning. *Hmm, is that where he really was?* He came home smelling like smoke and alcohol. He then took his sister and brother with him to the studio. They came home late, drunk, smelling of smoke and alcohol. I could not take it. I wasn't a drinker nor a smoker, so this really bothered me. The more I would complain, the more they all would stay out late. They blatantly disregarded everything I would say and tried to point the issues in my direction. That was when I became an outcast. When they went out together, they left me home alone with the kids.

After a while, I moved back home with my mother. I put my oldest daughter in school, and I began to have some peace of mind. Ricardo reluctantly came with me. My mother neither liked him, nor his family. She said she could feel something was not right with them, she just couldn't put her finger on the issue. We stayed there for a while and things got a little better. He became more focused, however, he wasn't happy. He said he felt like a prisoner. He felt as if his freedom was snatched from under his feet. He could not do whatever he wanted to do, therefore, he was extremely uncomfortable in my mother's house.

Shortly after Auntie Millie passed away, his parents said they needed his help and sent for him to move to Murphy, Texas. I did not want him to go but I could not say, "Don't go help your family, stay here with us." By this time his mother, father, one sister and a brother were all in Murphy trying to build a church and establish a home. Reluctantly I agreed for him to go with a plan we both agreed on. He was to go to Texas, help his parents get on their feet, then go two towns over to Dallas to start looking for a job, and establish a home for the kids and me to join him.

I never wanted to live with his family or any other family members again. There is nothing like having your own. The plan was for me to stay in New Jersey, work the two jobs seven days a week and save money. I was a full time newly hired employee at Hooper Hospital clinic, and worked at a Department store on the weekends. It just made sense for me to stay in NJ since the pay was higher. I was already holding down a good job with great benefits.

The money I was making would have been enough to fund his trip to Texas, so he could help his family, find a job and then look for a house. The kids would stay with me to continue their schooling until he was ready for us to join him. He agreed. I was a fool. On the day that he left, he took my oldest daughter out of school early. Yes, he kidnapped her and took her to Murphy with him. He did not call me, he did not tell anyone, did not warn me; she was just gone. I received a call from my neighbor who was scheduled to pick her up that afternoon saying that my baby girl was gone. She had gone to the school, as was customary, to pick her up and the school informed her that her father had already picked her up! I was terrified. I called Ricardo, but no answer. I called his mother, no answer. I called his father – you guessed it – no answer. I called everyone I could possibly think of who was related to them. No one would answer the phone. My heart was in my throat. My mom and grandmother were nervous wrecks. They yelled at me and threatened to call the police. I tried to remain calm and continued to be the voice of reason. I kept calling all night.

At around 1 A.M., my phone rang. It was my baby girl's voice. "Hi Mommy; I'm a country girl."

My face turned white; my heart dropped. I did not sleep all night and after hundreds of calls they finally had the decency to call me to tell me that they took her with them.

When I began to complain, the coy reply that came from his mother's lips was so insensitive: "Well is that Rocky's baby or what?" (Rocky was his nickname for Ricardo).

On one hand I was relieved that "pretty girl" was ok, but on the other hand, I was shocked that she asked me such a thing especially at that moment when I was petrified and worried that something horrible happened to my baby. "Yes, of course it is his baby," I said.

That was when Ricardo took the phone and said as calmly as ever, "She's here; we reached safely. It was a long trip, but we made it."

I was shocked, upset, disappointed, and offended all at once. I was so drained from worry, that I did not know how to respond. I simply asked, "Why didn't you call me to let me know that you were going to take her? Why didn't you answer the phone, leave me a message, or tell your family to give me a call or even call my family so we wouldn't worry?" I was so upset. I didn't even get to kiss my baby good-bye.

As he attempted to explain his point of view so many things began running in and out of my head:
"What if he gave me the wrong address and I never saw her again?"
"What if they are not who they say they are and harm her?"
"How do I know if he was telling me the truth?"
"Someone who claimed to love you and purposely hurt you by taking your child you gave birth to without regard to how you feel is not a particularly good person."

What was I going to do? That was the man I chose to marry. He just kidnapped my baby and refused to comfort me, or to inform me of her whereabouts. What was I going to do? By this time, it was three in the morning, and I had to go to work after staying up for almost 24 hours. It made no sense to go to sleep. I couldn't sleep anyway. Fighting back the tears, I asked the Lord a rhetorical question: "What did I do to deserve this?" The answer came back, "You married him."

Before I married Ricardo, I only prayed when I needed an answer to a troubling question, or when something unexpected happened, or when I wanted something specific.

I did not have a real relationship with the Lord, as I was a new Christian, a babe in Christ, and still on the milk of the Word. I wanted to talk to my heavenly Father, but I did not know how. I tried to pray the prayers I heard in church. I wanted to pray the right way without offending the Lord. I had to learn that prayer came from a penitent heart and not necessarily from a lot of words or from a spirit of self-righteousness.

The years ahead would teach me what true prayer was about, and learning to keep continuous communications with the Lord. I knew I had to get my baby back. I worked long shifts at both jobs and saved quite a bit of money. The clock was ticking, time was passing and my heart ached for my baby girl. She was in school down there and I did not want to interrupt her schedule, so I made the heart wrenching decision to let her stay.

I did, however, pressure my husband to move on to Dallas as planned, but his family would always find a reason why he needed to stay in Murphy. I even heard his father tell him several times that I was supposed to go where he said, and not the other way around. Of course, Ricardo's responses to me were, "They still need me here." Months passed; he was not working. He continued to hang out with his brother, and spent our hard earned savings, earmarked for a house, on things like drinking, smoking and God knows what else.

Twice I tried to pay some bills and the account was near depletion. I opened a separate account so I could see and control where the money was going. I didn't know if that was the right thing to do but I did not want to play "Bobo" the fool anymore. I confronted him about all the money that was drained from the account. His response was that his parents needed a few thousand dollars, so he helped them out. I didn't know if he was telling the truth but I was working seven days a week with overtime with little or no sleep, and saving money to buy a house. Meanwhile, he spent it faster than I could make it, so I closed the account!! One week later he called me and said he could not get any money from the bank. I told him to get a job, and find a place to stay because I wasn't going to Texas to live in his parent's house.

Just about a year after we had that discussion, according to his own timetable, he was ready to do the right thing. He found a job and rented a house for us to move into. We officially relocated and took the long journey to a Dallas suburb. That was a big mistake! I really had no choice. I was either staying in New Jersey in my mother's house living with one daughter or moving to Texas to be with my husband and our other daughter. I was torn! I decided to quit my good job because I loved my family and I wanted us to be together as one. When I thought about it, I realized that it was God who gave me that job in the first place, so why wouldn't he give me another? I honored my husband's wishes to join him and I thought I was being a good wife. Unbeknownst to me, the enemy had plans for me and I was playing right into his hands.

When I got to Texas everything changed. My husband was drinking and smoking a lot, hanging out with his brother until all hours of the night. They were either in the street, at a friend's house, or at our house. I complained about them hanging out and smoking in our house because I didn't drink or smoke. In addition, the children had school early every morning. Nevertheless, my wishes were ignored and every night he, his friends, and his brother smoked, drank, sang, and played loud secular music. I asked him to work with me because we had to get up in the morning. I begged him to at least cut it short so that we could rest. I told him that the kids did not need to see, smell, or hear what was going on in our house, but he would not stop. His brother increased the volume of the music and they would scream and sing at the top of their lungs. I would often ask myself, "Lord, what did I get myself into?" The answer came back, "You took the ring!"

I should point out that I did not know anyone in the entire state or the one neighboring it. I was pretty much alone – just me and my kids. His family only included me in their lives when they wanted me to do something for them or to save face in church. I was always the outsider, along with any girlfriend his brother had at the time. It was a very lonely life. I would go to work, put on a smile and function to the glory of God. I am not saying I was a saint because I wasn't. I was a sinner saved by grace according to Romans 3:23, *For all have sinned, and come short of the glory of God.* No pedestal for me!

Things were quite tough to deal with. Only my continuous conversations with the Lord and the knowledge that He loved me and was with me that kept me going. If I did not have that relationship, I probably would have killed myself or my husband. I had to believe that since God was leading me, He protected and covered me as well. I had to believe that He brought me through my trials. There was no other way. Who else could I turn to? My mother? She couldn't help me, and if she knew what I was dealing with, I would have to fight off an army of cousins, brothers, and friends from doing great bodily harm to Ricardo. My neighbors? I could only smile and wave at them because my husband's jealousy was so out of control. I had no one to turn to but God. All I had was Jesus: Psalm 46:1 encouraged me. *God was my refuge and strength, a very present help in trouble.*

By this point in time I began to suspect that he was having some mental issues. Maybe it was schizophrenia. He would say and do things and moments later he would say he had not said or done them. The things that came out of his mouth were so strange and bizarre that I would often ask him: "Ricardo, did you hear what you just said?" Sometimes he would even laugh at what he said because it was so bizarre. He would say things like some people told him that they saw me sleeping with the guy at the bodega on the back-room floor on a Tuesday at 3:00 pm. When I asked him who the people were, he could not tell me. He would say, "Just people." He said I was sleeping with my neighbor's husband, his brother, his aunt, his father, my boss, the guy in the bodega. His bizarre response came because one day I simply asked him if he had a CD of a certain gospel artist. He also had me sleeping with some nameless guy on his job whom I never met and likely never would meet because of the high security at the facility. I was not even allowed to go past the guarded gate or even go through the metal detector so there was no way for me to break into his job and sleep with this mysterious person. This is how ridiculous he sounded; his mind was going fast. He kept losing jobs left and right because of his paranoid state. I did not know who I was going to come home to each night. His personality changed by the hour. I never knew who I was talking to.

One night after work I was lying in bed, and he came in. He was as sweet as honey like the man I married. He said, "Good evening my beloved, how was your day?" Then he kissed me on the cheek and walked out the room. Five minutes later he came back into the room with his finger in my face screaming, "I should kill you!!!" He left the room and was peeking at me shaking his finger as if he wanted to say something but just turned and walked away. I didn't know what was going through his mind, but I was afraid. I prayed, and prayed, and prayed to God. "Lord, I don't understand what is going on. I don't know what to do. Please tell me what to do."

I tried several times to get Ricardo to go to counseling or to see a doctor, but he refused. He did not think anything was wrong with him. He said I was the crazy one, and I was the one who had the problem. Some mentally ill people don't think or realize that they have a problem. When he calmed down, I told him I was feeling stressed, and I felt like I was losing my mind. I wanted to see a counselor and maybe check myself into the hospital. I asked him to go with me. He was more than happy to go and made a list of things that he thought would get me committed to the hospital. I figured that once we got there and the doctor observed his strange behavior maybe they would get him help.

We went to the appointment and just as I thought, he started telling the doctor all this crazy stuff so that eventually the doctor's attention was now focused on him and not on me. The doctor listened attentively and realized that he had to try to help him. When my husband left the room I told the doctor about my husband's strange behaviors and that

I was concerned. He indicated that he had already noticed his unusual behavior. As soon as Ricardo came back into the room the doctor was able to discern that he had some challenges. He was constantly pacing, talking extremely loud and aggressively. He asked Ricardo to make an appointment to see him. He became really agitated, refused to set the appointment and demanded that we leave. We left. I tried to calm him down, but to no avail. He took me home and immediately stormed out the house.

This was a regular pattern of his so that I would be trapped at home and couldn't go anywhere. Even when we had two cars, he would give my car to his brother or his father leaving me stuck at home with no way to get around. He would take my car keys from the dresser or out of my bag and drove away for hours. The enemy was trying to infiltrate my home and had his minions chip away at us. He was already wreaking havoc on my husband and now he was trying to chip away at me.

His brother started using drugs and developed a serious habit. He took my personal belongings or things he thought could benefit him. None of them respected me, my house or how I felt. I had to pray heavily. Things were getting worse with my husband acting crazy, and his "friend" and brother following close behind. I believed they were hatching a plan to get rid of me. I would hear his "friend" say things like

"No one can be that happy all the time." His brother did not like me anyway so nothing good about me would come from his mouth. This was an exhausting time for me and I was pregnant with our third child. When he found out it was a boy, he slowed down with the crazy talk. He was nicer and did not threaten me as much – but he was still crazy.

When my baby boy was almost one year old, he lost it again and started fighting with me again, yelling and screaming, talking crazy about the people I was sleeping around with: men, women and animals. Everything that would come to his mind he would put on me as the scapegoat and that it was my fault. He accused me of even sleeping with people I never even met. Then he started making up people and said I was sleeping with them also. He said the people told him this, but he could never tell me who the people were.

His threats were getting worse. His brother purchased a gun and treated it as if it was a new toy. They were very reckless and waved it around too freely for me. All the threats he kept throwing my way made me extremely nervous. His brother already threatened his wife with his new gun, holding it to her head. I knew my time would be coming soon. Ricardo brought a case of bullets and slammed them down on my dresser and told me that they had my name on them, then walked out of the room. I checked, my name was not on them. Of course, in his mind they were marked with my name. I had no place else to go and he was my husband.

I was trying to work things out. I did not want to get a divorce like my mom did. I was in constant prayer day and night asking the Lord to help me. To tell me what to do. I was committed and I wanted to try to help him. I loved him. He was my husband, but he did not act like it. He would often make reference to the bullets on the dresser, pick them up and smile menacingly rubbing his hands together saying, "I'm going to kill me a nigger. I can't wait to get my gun." I told his mother but she just brushed me off and said I was making stuff up. I told his father who took it a little more seriously.

Early one morning he and his dad went for a drive and did not come back at a reasonable time – in my estimation. I thought maybe they went to his parents' house, but they did not answer the phone. I called at 6 P.M. and still no one answered the phone. When someone finally picked up, they said that Pops was not there and then hung up. I called back and asked if they returned, but the response was the same, "No they hadn't returned". Surprisingly, it turned out that Ricardo admitted himself into the hospital, and they did not have the decency to tell me. Why didn't they tell me? Would I just forget I was married and that I had a troubled husband who was seeking help from his father? It was a weekend and so I went to see him in the hospital. He was drugged and drooling on himself. Naked in a room all alone. I tried to talk to him but he was incoherent and slurred his words. I wiped away the drool and asked the nurse what was wrong with him. They had no answers for me that night and told me to go home and try to rest and come back the next day when the doctor would be there. I called Pops and asked him why he couldn't just tell me that he was committed. I would have wanted to be there for his care; after all, I was his wife. His answer was cold and impersonal. "You asked me for help, so I helped you."

I went back to the hospital the next day to find out that he was taken to the main mental hospital in Dallas because he became aggressive and fought the guard. Of course, the family blamed me for going to see him and suggested that his outburst with the guards was all my fault. According to his parents, I should not have gone to see him until the medication was fully in his system. Ricardo spent another four weeks in the main psychiatric hospital in Dallas. His parents went to see him frequently but would not allow me to go. The excuse was that I triggered his episodes.

When I was finally allowed to go see him, I asked the doctor to explain to me what the issues were with him. He told me that he had paranoid schizophrenia, and border-line psychotic disorder. Then he pulled me to the side and suggested that I leave, get out of town and leave. I was confused. I didn't tell his family what the doctor said, but I'm sure he had a good reason. When I went home, I realized I had nowhere to go with no money and no transportation. I was stuck and I would not leave without my children. I had to stay.

I did not understand his parents' reasoning or logic for some of the things they did or said or even how they treated me. They blamed me for everything. If he did not eat, even if the plate of food was sitting right in front of him and he refused to eat it, they blamed me. If the house was not tidy because the kids and Ricardo *tore it up* while I was working two jobs, then it was my fault. Everything was my fault. They looked down on me. If I did something wrong they would tell their daughters not to be like me instead of coming to me in love and sharing with me the correct way to handle or do something. On one occasion my brother-in-law kidnapped my son from his mother's house. This is my only son whom I earnestly prayed to God for. He was missing with my son for an entire week. I could not eat, I could not drink, I could not sleep. I may have had an hour of sleep per day and that was only because I cried myself to sleep. Their concern was for their grown son who kidnapped their two-year-old grandson – their only grandson – their namesake. I nearly lost my mind. I sat in a rocking chair crying and rocking. Every car that passed by, I would run to the door hoping it was them bringing my baby boy home. On the seventh day I lost it. I had a breakdown when they came to the door without my son. I could not stop crying uncontrollably. My father-in-law had to pray for my mind. I could not stop crying and shaking, just thinking about all the things that could be happening or perhaps had happened to my son. After he prayed, from that moment on, I had peace. God assured me that he was ok. I stopped crying and shortly thereafter they received a call that someone saw my brother-in-law driving down a particular street. They all rushed in the car and brought my little boy home. He was ok; no harm was done to him. I had him checked out by the doctor and all was well. I could breathe again until the next episode. It was only by God's grace I made it through. The Devil almost had my mind, but God stepped in just in the nick of time. God is a mind regulator, a keeper, and He is eternally faithful.

I did not allow his mother to watch my son again for a long time unless I was there or close by. This wasn't the first time he kidnapped my baby boy. Yes, there was a second time! This time my brother-in-law disappeared for three days with both of his nephews. Ricardo and I were able to cut him off with our car when he was trying to get away at a gas station. We took the boys out of the car and immediately took them to the hospital to have a doctor check them out and he told us that they were ok. Now, we needed to pay for this doctor's visit and so I asked Ricardo to get his nephew's insurance card to pay for the hospital visit. Ricardo's mother got terribly angry with me and made it seem as if I made up the story about her son kidnapping the boys. She said it was all foolishness and that since I took them to the hospital to be checked out it was my responsibility. I never understood his family's logic. Again, instead of causing friction in the family I just paid the bill out of my pocket. I didn't really have the money, but I had to live among them and I had no one else to turn to.

I tried to stay away from the entire family as best as I could. I wanted time to teach my children right from wrong, humility, integrity, honesty and all the good virtues in the Bible while they were still young, pliable and it was easy to instill a good, godly foundation. The Bible tells us to, *Train up a child in the way he should go, and when he is old, he will not depart from it.* Proverbs 22:6. I always wanted them to know I loved them, but would not tolerate lying, stealing, foolishness at home or anywhere else. I never wanted my love for them to blind me from their wrongdoing.

I remember, as my son was getting older, that I had to teach him a serious lesson for stealing. I took him to the local police station because he stole our rent money and had the nerve to take it to school. I whipped his behind really well and took him to the precinct. I told him that if he ever stole again and lied to me, I would leave him with the cops. I told him that I loved him dearly and as my only son he was dear to my heart, but I would not live in the same house with a liar and a thief. He probably still remembers that whipping, but he never stole from me or anyone else, as far as I know.

If that was not enough, Ricardo started up again talking out of his mind. He would snatch my Bible from me and throw it across the room screaming at me, "THERE IS NO GOD! HE DOES NOT EXIST!" That was when I told him that he was going down a dark path that I could not follow. The more I tried to help him the angrier he would get; the more violent he would become. Once, while I was pregnant with our last child, he pushed me so hard that I fell on a rocky driveway and scraped up my hands and knees. To him it was funny, so he laughed about it. Other times he would not smoke all day, but as soon as we were in a closed space, he'd light up a cigarette and keep the windows locked so I could not have any fresh air to breathe. One time my dad came to visit me and he did that in the car. No matter how much I asked him, nicely, to put out the cigarette, he would not, and instead he would light them up back-to-back like a chain smoker. My dad told him to respect his wife's wishes. He eventually listened, for the moment.

I did not know how much more I could take. Having to deal with the constant threats, the rough treatment, the blatant disregard for my life and well-being, the tiresome personality changes, the violent fits, the constant accusations, and blaming me for everything. How much more could one person take? This was truly my "Job experience." It was only God's encouragement through studying his Word, especially the Psalm, *He will not leave you, nor forsake you.* I knew I needed to encourage myself through the Word and through worship (music). God encouraged me through Matthew 6:25-34. I also listened to the words of good, encouraging gospel music, such as Yolanda Adams' song, *The Battle is Not Yours it's the Lord's.* The quiet times I spent driving to and from work gave me some moments of relief. I was mentally and physically drained. I prayed for God to take me away. I tried every divine intervention given to me as well as earthly interventions from doctors and medical books that I could find. I was about to give up when my husband brought a butcher knife with him to bed and put it under his pillow. I was done! I prayed to God, "Father, I give up. I can't do this anymore; if it's meant to be my time then let your will be done." I sat up in bed. I could see his shadow with the knife raised up in the air and I could hear him trying to muster up his strength as he got closer to me. I turned around, looked at him, and he put the knife behind his back and left the room. He did not sleep in the room but stayed in the living room playing his guitar all night. It was truly God who stopped him that night because the shadow that warned me was facing the wrong way! The light from my night table would shine on that side of the room, and when it was on, *my* shadow would reflect on his side of the room but, on that night, *his* shadow reflected on my side of the room. I was able to see him creeping up behind me. God is so good. He was my protector, my shield and my buckler. *Goodness and mercy shall follow me all the days of my life*, Psalm 23.

There were so many horrifying stories I could write about my "Job experience" with this man. He tried to rip the baby out of my womb and almost caused me to lose her. I was able to fight him off, but I spotted and had really bad cramps for days. Another time he went into a rage and I tried to protect the kids, so I told them to go to their room and close the door, but they forgot their baby brother. So I ran into his room, grabbed him and pushed him in the room with the girls! I told them not to open the door until I told them to, no matter what. By the time I closed the door Ricardo was upon me. He was mumbling something I could not understand, but he was clearly angry.

He weighed about 145-150 pounds, and stood almost six feet tall. I was about 140 pounds and almost nine months pregnant when he grabbed me by the throat and held me up against the wall with one hand saying, "I'm going to kill you!"

I grabbed his hand and said, "I can't breathe, stop!"

I was fighting, but that only took away my breath faster. Things were starting to get dim and my head felt light. I could hear my heart beating in my ears. I begin to pray, "Father, I need your help. Help me!" The answer came,

"Be very still." I stopped fighting. I took as many slow, deep breaths as I could with his hand around my neck. I closed my eyes and stayed very still. He lowered me to the floor and loosened his grip. I took a slow breath in and opened my eyes. He proceeded to sit on top of my big pregnant belly and tried to choke the life out of me. I held my breath. I could hear my heart slowing down in my ears. I closed my eyes because he did not even look like my husband anymore; he looked possessed, wild and ungodly, but I still held my breath and laid very still – limp like a wet noodle. I did not move, I did not breathe, I did not flinch, I just laid there still. He continued to sit on my belly and even the baby was extremely still in my belly. I could hear my heartbeat becoming slower and slower. I felt my body relax. I was just still. He finally got up and went towards the living room. I cracked my eyes open to see what he was doing. I did not know if he was going to get a knife or what he had planned. As soon as he turned the corner into the living room I jumped up, told the kids to open the door and ran inside. He heard me jump up and started to run down the hall to catch me. I just made it in by a hair's-breadth. He tried to unscrew the doorknob and I pushed the bed against the door. Then he ran outside to the window. The kids were crying, and I tried my best to comfort them. The window was locked so I was sure that he could not get in. He came back inside and tried to break down the door, but he couldn't. I didn't even have a phone with me to call the police. My neighbors, all police and retired detectives could not hear our cries for help because they were too far away. They were so close but yet so far. Ricardo got tired of trying to get in and jumped in his car and sped away.

I grabbed the kids and put them in my car. I had nowhere to go, no family but his. I could not have any friends without him being insanely jealous and accusing me of sleeping with them, even if they were females, plus he took all my money. I had none in the bank and no money I put aside. His family would shame me for putting money away, and he would take it all from me. There was little gas in the car, and there I was stuck and stranded. I went to his parents' house, explained to them what happened, and they told me to go into the room and lie down. A few hours later he came to his parents' house. They sent him right in to me. "Go lie down with her," and they closed the door. They sent him in and closed the door! My God! After everything I told them. I could not believe it. I told them that their son tried to kill me and their unborn grandchild, and the same day they told him where I was and sent him in the room with me. Were they trying to get me killed? I did not understand it. That night I did not sleep, and he laid there right up under me with his leg draped over me. If I moved, he would wake up, "Where do you think you are going?" There was no rest for me that night. I thought about getting the kids and jumping in the car and just driving till the gas ran out, but they lived in the

woods with bears and all kinds of animals. Also, there was
no way for me to move without this man tracking my every
breath. I was not leaving my babies. His mother locked them
in the room with her. I had no choice; I had to stay. In a few
hours I would have to put on a good face and go to work
with bruises on my neck and arms. I felt trapped and like
it was only a matter of time before I would be taken out of
this world. My only consolation was God. II Corinthians
tells me, *to be absent from the body, is to be present with the Lord.*
II Timothy 4:7 encouraged me to know that *I fought a good
fight, I have finished my course, and I have kept the faith.*

I was committed. I did everything I could possibly do to save
my husband and my marriage. I did my best to be a good
wife, but he did not want me. I gave everything – the only
thing left was my life. I prayed, "Lord let your will be done;
if this is my lot in life then let it be. My life is in your hands.
I am tired, I am weak, weary and worn. I can't go on any
further. If you don't help me no one can."

Later that week was the final straw. It was on "baby girl's"
birthday. I was nine months pregnant with my youngest
daughter. I came home from work and he was home with
the kids. I knew something would happen. I didn't even
want to go in the house, but I dragged myself inside. I had
to put on my "trusty mask" for my kids so they would not
be afraid of what was going on in the house. I tried really

hard to shield everything from them. I did not want them to think their father was a monster. For the few things they did see, I told them he was sick and needed to take his medication. I came into the house and the kids greeted me at the door, as always. Ricardo looked me up and down and said, "Beloved." I replied with a "hello" and went into the room to change out of my uniform.

He said that he had invited the family to come over to celebrate our daughter's birthday. I was really tired, and I did not want to entertain. I was nine months pregnant; I just had this ordeal where he tried to choke the life out of me and our unborn child. I just got home from work and he proceeded to tell me that his family was coming over for a birthday party. The house was a wreck, the kids were a mess, and we had no birthday party supplies. How was I going to pull this off? I took a deep breath and walked over to the bedroom as fast as I could. I was having back pains from standing on my feet all day. As I was rushing around the room trying to get dressed before his family arrived, Ricardo walked in and began watching me. All of a sudden he punched me in the back of the head pushing me forward into the closet door. I got up and tried to leave. I saw him coming toward me and turned so he would not hit me in the face or my stomach. He hit me in the ear so hard that it began ringing. He then grabbed both my arms and threw me down on the bed and said, "I could kill you." As I laid on the bed, he started toward me with that deranged look in his eyes again. His entire countenance changed; his demeanor was not the same man – that was not Ricardo. He walked over to me slowly and I kicked him in the stomach. That angered him! He tried to grab me and I fought for my life and the life of my unborn child. I started throwing stuff at him and he blocked them and lounged after me. He pulled me by my hair and tried to wrap his hands around my neck. I bit his hand. He grabbed after me to get a hold of me, but I would not let him. We tussled on the bed. I tried to protect the baby in my stomach with one hand and fight him off with the other. In one of our previous fights, I broke my right arm, and a steel plate was put in it to help it mend. He was coming down on me hard and trying to hold me down. I took my right arm and swung it around as hard as I could. He turned slightly to the right and I thrashed him across his back to get him off me. I figured my arm was not likely to break again. That hurt him and he backed down and went into the living room. My right arm was in so much pain, it swelled up and I put on some clothes and went to the car. He followed me and jumped in the car with me. I was crying from pain.

"Get away from me!" I got out of the car screaming and cry-ing, "Stay away from me." I could not move my arm without pain. I thought I broke it again because it was the same kind of excruciating pain as before. I did not want him to touch me! I did not want him near me! I did not want him to talk to me! I was done! I yelled, "You will not get another chance to kill me!"

His father drove up and heard me crying in pain. He saw that my arm was swollen and red. He said he would take me to the emergency room. I told him to keep Ricardo away from me. He took me to the hospital. I refused to speak to anyone but the doctor. Pops stayed with me; they asked if I wanted him to leave but I wanted him to stay. The doctor asked me what happened. I was a little reluctant with Pops there, but I wanted him to hear it in front of someone else so there was no excuse for Ricardo's action and no blame on me. I told the doctor everything, even about the fight where I broke my arm the first time. The good news was that my arm was not broken again, but it was bruised right down into the bone and the plate was slightly displaced.

While I was at the hospital, I spoke to a domestic violence counselor who asked me if I wanted to get away. Absolutely yes, but I needed help to make that happen. They told me that I could be transferred to an undisclosed location straight from the hospital for my safety and the safety of the women and children who lived there. I told her I wanted to go but not without my children. If I couldn't get my children, I was willing to go back into that crazy life. So they arranged for me to fill out a report and an officer in a squad car arrested my husband and kept him at the precinct long enough for me to gather the kids and a few belongings. I threw everything in my jeep and followed the counselor to the shelter. That was one of the hardest things I had ever done.

I don't believe God created me to be abused and tortured by that man. I had to be strong for my children, for myself and for my unborn child.

Being in the shelter was so hard, but I put on the happy mask for the kids. It was an emotional roller coaster, but I hung on tight. I was dealing with hormonal issues due to the pregnancy and I was in horrible pain from my arm. This was a very stressfully painful and unbearable time for me, but I had to do it. We stayed in a small room with four other families where we shared cooking and cleaning chores. There were lots of rules for everyone's safety. I could not even call my mom or anyone I knew to let them know that I was ok. I cried all night till morning when it was time to get the kids up and ready for school. I could not even shower myself because my arm was in so much pain. "Baby girl" had to help me bathe because I could not support myself with my arm and I was off balance with my big belly. I could not see my feet to tie my shoes, so the girls had to help me get dressed. After I dropped the kids off to school I would go back to the shelter and slowly do my chores with one arm and a big belly as best as I could. Sometimes the other women would feel sorry for me and help me out. I was depressed. I could not eat or drink. I could not do anything but cry day and night. I did not want to do anything but just stare out the window and talk to God. I knew the other women heard me crying late at night. For weeks that was my routine. I just cried till I could not shed any more tears. I wanted to die, but who would be there for my children? No one would take care of them like I would. So, I just lingered on in a dark haze. Talking to God. I was not angry with God, I was angry with myself for allowing myself to be put in the position of mental, physical, financial and emotional abuse. I was angry at Ricardo for betraying me. I was angry at his family for blaming me for his actions. I was hurt because he betrayed me. I was with this man for 18 years of my life. For 18 years I put up with him and all the trials, ups and downs, good and bad and he just betrayed me. Like I did not mean anything to him at all. At that point God was the only one I could turn to. I would ask him many questions throughout this time. For example, if Ricardo was not the one for me why would He allow me to marry him. The answer was simple. Like the narrative of David and Bathsheba, I wanted it and He gave me what I wanted and used it to bring me closer to Him, and to keep the promise that was made to his parents and grandparents to carry on. Ricardo had not married anyone else because there was something in his bloodline – the promise that God made to his family. What was my purpose in this? God trusted me with the precious gifts of four lives to raise and teach them about His ways. All the gifts God blessed Ricardo with are in these four children. I had so many questions and very few answers. Then she moved. My heart was overwhelmed. She had not moved in weeks and she finally moved! She was still alive! The darkness from those dark days did not take her.

I praised God and thanked him for my children – every one of them. They are a blessing to my life, and I couldn't imagine life without them. I started to feel a little better.

After not eating for nearly a week or two I started to nibble here and there. I thank God for his grace and mercy and the trials I went through with Ricardo. I would not have made it without God in my life. Those trials were put in my life to make me stronger, to build my relationship with God. So he could prove to me without a shadow of a doubt who He is, and to whom I belong. I know that He loves me. I went from knowing of God, to calling him my Heavenly Father. A good father who cares for me and has my best interest at heart. The seclusion, the accusations, the constant blaming, the betrayal, the loneliness, the threats, the mental episodes, and the disappointments made me realize that it was really, really a difficult time for me, but by God's grace I made it. We moved back to New Jersey.

MANY YEARS LATER, LIFE WAS STILL HARD but manageable while raising four active kids alone with one in elementary school, two in junior high, and one in high school. I had no help, so I worked pretty hard trying to make ends meet and to support my family. I worked lots of over-time and some Saturdays. I had no time for anything called relaxation – just a life filled with *hurrying*! Hurry up to get to classes; hurry up to get to church services; hurry up to get to work on time; just hurry up! We began attending a Bethel Community Missions church in Hawthorne, NJ regularly on Sundays with an occasional mid-week Bible study.

I began to have a lot of problems with my co-workers. These issues affected my health and I lost 20 lbs in three months. The enemy was distracting me; this was not a pleasant time for me. I was losing focus on the important things in life and on God. He had just miraculously brought me through extreme distress and in my hurry to do what He wanted me to do, I forgot about the most important part. I forgot Him! God had shown me a part of His plan for my life, but in bits and pieces. I could see the end and some of the middle, but I did not know how or where to begin. I knew where I wanted to go, but not how to get there. The enemy was not making it easy for me either.

So to bring this journey current and up to date, let me share an incident that happened in my life about over seven years ago. My children and I were happy in Bethel. They found a place where they could minister and grow in God. One Sunday after Church, I was in a hurry to gather the kids so that we could hurry home and get ready for school and for work on Monday. When I could not find my second daughter, who was a social butterfly, I began rushing from place to place looking for her, but without success. Someone told me she was in the main sanctuary which was across the street from the social hall.

I wanted to hurry to cross the street but, In my haste to cross the street, I couldn't move as quickly as I wanted because of the traffic. I waited for the traffic to clear so I could get across, but it was heavy. I made a third attempt to cross, noticing that the traffic light was in my favor. The light was obviously red but vehicles were still edging along. A bus blocked my way, so I had to wait. I saw an SUV from the corner of my left eye and he seemed to be slowing down. After all, the light was red and the cars were stopped in front of him. He had to stop. He should stop! So, I waited patiently for the bus to go by so I could cross. I noticed the young man driving the SUV was not stopping. I saw his hands in the air waving as if to say, "No, no, no, no." So, I started backing up to move out of the street but I was not fast enough. The next thing I knew he was on me. The wheel caught my shoe and I could not back up anymore. I was stuck! I closed my eyes and held my breath. CRACK!!

I remember hearing words whispered to me to breathe, let go, and rest. Then I heard noises of people screaming and talking. I heard the sounds of cars and sirens. Everything was still blurry. I saw that I was stuck between two cars. I could not see my legs. I did not feel anything until I tried to move them. Oh! The pain came rushing in. I shut my eyes tightly and held myself up in my arms. I could hear the people whispering, and I saw the horror on their faces through my hair which was now covering my face. I held my head down, and I tried to breathe slowly and intentionally to ease the pain. I could not look at their faces. I knew I was going to be ok, but I could not look at their faces as fear and horror surrounded me and stared back at me. If I looked I would lose it. God already told me to breathe, let go, and rest and that is what I intended to do. "Don't lose focus – keep your head down and breathe, pray, breathe, pray." People kept peeking in my face, I guess from the shock, but I closed my eyes and breathed and prayed for God's mercy and the grace to go through.

It seemed like forever. If I did not move, I would not be in pain. Then an officer came and told the occupants of the car in front that I was pinned, and they were to move the vehicle forward. The cars pulled apart and I heard the officer say, "Hold." I tried to lift myself to my feet with my arms, but when I looked at my legs, they were flat like sheets of paper and I could not stand. I shut my eyes again. Not because I could not bear to watch, but I had to stay focused on God's grace and mercy. I prayed continually without ceasing. I remember everyone staring at me and the look of horror on the faces of the people who were on the bus as it slowly passed by. All I could say was, "Grace and mercy." Lord have mercy on me. I remember a woman who stood behind me and held me up. She bore my weight from my arms so I could rest. I was so incredibly grateful. I was able to let go and rest just like God said, breathe, let go and rest. I was hoping she would put me on the ground, but she didn't. I was in a lot of pain and it was getting worse hanging there. I felt myself getting antsy and agitated because of the pain. So, I asked as humbly and as gently as I could for her to kindly put me on the ground. The ground was hard and hot. I did not care. I whispered and repeated the words, "Grace and Mercy." That was all I could get out. I started to shiver, it was no longer hot, but now it was cold. Everything was cold. I could feel my warm blood turning cold. My lips were dry, and my tongue stuck to the roof of my mouth. People were scrambling all around me and I covered my face with my hands and prayed for grace and mercy.

Here's a side note: I thought I heard my pastor's voice, but I was in an uncertain daze. In service that morning they had announced that he and his wife would be leaving immediately after church to go away on vacation. I was told by someone on the scene that they heard the commotion and came to check on me. I vaguely remember an officer telling my pastor to step back and to leave the scene. I imagined that I glimpsed his wife in the background with her arms folded – I knew she was praying. About a week later I was told the full story of what really happened with my pastor. The officer wouldn't allow him to come close to me and pray. All he wanted to do was to pray for me. The officer did not care who he was because he wasn't next of kin. He told my pastor, who was also my bishop – that if he insisted on getting close to me, he would arrest him. He pushed him aside and told him to leave the scene. My pastor reported him to the police chief and that officer was relocated to another precinct.

Back to the scene. I heard a familiar voice on my right. I reached up and grabbed his hand, straining to focus my eyes. My eyes were blurry and painful from all the crying and from squeezing them closed so tightly – they felt sore. It was a Brother from my church, I said Hi. I remembered I had money in my hand, and I gave it to him and asked him to give it to my Auntie. I remembered him helping the paramedics to put the board under my back. It was so painful, all I could whisper was, "Jesus!" The pain shot all through my body, and the burning ran down my legs and felt like the skin on my legs were sliding off like loose stockings that wouldn't stay up! When they finally got me on the stretcher, I saw Bishop in front by the ambulance door praying. That made me feel better. It was a bumpy ride and very painful.

There was so much going on, but I could not tell what. I realized that my clothes were cut open going one way and another. IV needles and bags of fluids were tossed on top of me. Then I remember being pushed through one corridor to another corridor. I was in the hospital. All this time in excruciating pain. Finally, someone gave me something for pain. It started to slowly numb the pain and then it kicked in and things started to go black.

I woke up in a cat scan or MRI chamber, not sure. I was inside a noisy machine in extreme pain with burning and shooting pain in the whole lower half of my body. The pain was so bad I could not stop crying. The nurse came to ask me what's wrong. I told her I was in pain. I was in and out of consciousness. I remember I was in a corridor, and a figure standing over me. I could not make out what they were saying. I rubbed my eyes and strained to focus. It was the doctor. He asked me, "How do you feel?" I heard my mother's voice through the door over my head. I looked up at the doors and then looked at the doctor. He asked, "Is that your Mom?" I nodded. He opened the door and they wheeled me into another corridor with some of the saints and Mommy. Both my legs were broken. I had a tibial-fibular fracture on both legs and the right leg had an open fracture. The doctor explained to me that they put plates and screws in both legs.

They said I was a good candidate because of my age and health. They did not know if I would be able to walk again. It was too soon to tell.

While I was in the hospital, I couldn't wrap my mind around the fact that it was possible that I may never walk again. What? So, I decided not to think about it. I had many well-wishers and visitors who kept my spirits up. The funny thing is a lot of the visitors who came to encourage and wish me well, I ended up encouraging them instead. Don't get me wrong; I appreciated their kind gestures, but I was in a mental and spiritual place where I accepted my situation and decided to completely trust the Lord. Even those sharing the room with me, I tried to encourage them. You see, God had already let me know I was going to be alright. He had already brought me through some tough times, therefore, I already knew what it was like to have a broken bone with screws and a plate holding the ligaments, tendons and muscles together. If He could do it for me then I knew he would do it for me again. I have faith in God's Word that declares in Isaiah 53:5, *And with his stripes we are healed.* Also in Matthew 18:3, Jesus said, *Verily I say unto you, except ye be converted, and become as little children, ye shall not enter into the kingdom of heaven.* I trusted Him and I believed His Word. Why would He tell me I would be ok if He was not going to make it so? Just to take Him at his Word. He's not a man that he should lie, as it says in Numbers 23:19. Just believe without giving it a second thought just as a child would. Now it may not come as you expect, but it shall come. Even if it does not come, God is still God. Anyway, God's choice is always the best way. I can go on and on with inspiring scriptures but let's continue.

Even in the hospital God did not leave me. Whenever I felt a little down, he would send someone to cheer me up. I was still in a lot of pain and I could not use my legs. The hospital kept me for two weeks because I could not go home. I lived on a second floor walkup and my apartment was too narrow for a wheelchair. I was informed I needed to go to a skilled facility, but none of the rehabs would take me. This was extremely stressful, not having a place to go. One hour before they were to kick me out of the hospital, I took the matter to the Lord in prayer. "Lord, you know I can't go home yet. I can't go up the stairs and no one can carry me. Even if I did get someone to carry me upstairs, I wouldn't be able to move about in the house with the wheelchair and, Lord you know that I can't even stand up! You know what I need. They are about to kick me out of the hospital, and I have nowhere to go. I need your help!" Just then a nurse came in and said, "We found a rehab for you!" I said, "Thank you," and I gave the Lord Praise.

The rehab I was sent to was in an area in Hawthorne that was extremely far from my house and for my children to come and visit me, but it was a lovely facility. I healed quickly and was able to go home after three months of therapy. In no way did it mean that I was out of the woods. I had many challenges such as the visiting staff not wanting to help me. Some of them were insensitive enough to tell me that whatever I asked them to do, I should get up and go get it for myself. Others would not assist me in going to the bathroom. But thank God that for every mean attendant there were those who graciously and professionally attended to my needs. The main nurse's aide who took care of me treated me with care as if I were her child. She also encouraged me. My physical therapist was great, kind and quite a hard worker. She made me work very hard to achieve my goal and I pushed her to let me work harder. It was not easy, in fact, it was very painful, but I pushed forward, and I would not quit.

Today life is getting better. I still have my challenges, but God is the same yesterday, today, tomorrow and forever. He's the one constant in my life that keeps me going. Currently I'm working with a company I enjoy, living in a beautiful apartment with my family and my new husband whom I love and adore. He loves and adores me as well – that story is a blessing set up by God – worthy of telling, but for another time. Until then be blessed by the Lord and continue to praise Him for His goodness in your life.

THE AUTHORS

Rev. David Winston Anderson is the Senior Pastor of RH Ministries located in Red Hook, Brooklyn. In 1992, Pastor Anderson began working in the Jail Ministry. In June 1997 he was ordained as Rev. David Anderson and later installed as Pastor of RH Ministries. Today Pastor Anderson continues his work with those incarcerated as a Social Work Transporter/Investigator for the Legal Aid Society of Nassau County and as a Registered Nassau County Chaplain. Pastor Anderson has a passion for bringing the Word of God to those locked down but not locked out. Pastor Anderson and his wife, Linda, reside in West Hempstead, New York and are the proud parents of five children and have seven grandchildren.

Dr. Linda Delores Anderson is the wife of Pastor David W. Anderson of RH Ministries. She received her Doctorate in Theology from Anchor Theological Seminary in June 2016. Her passion is for people to come to know the truth of God's Word, experience the love of Jesus Christ and walk in the purpose that God has for them. Her favorite scripture is Jeremiah 29:11 and she is a firm believer that in God you can have a new beginning. Linda resides in West Hempstead, NY with her husband. They are the proud parents of five wonderful children, seven precious grandchildren.

Carly P. Bushelle is an author, educator and mentor with a passion for owning her truth. Coming face to face with the hardest truths is an essential part of her storytelling style and she is grateful for the opportunity to share her experiences.

Rev. Beverly Morrison Caesar is an ordained minister at Bethel Gospel Tabernacle. She founded ZizaCreative Publishing Company to assist authors in fulfilling their dreams at an affordable rate, ensuring a professional product. She has authored two books: *Experiencing The 25th Hour* and *3 Decades Later.* Beverly is a conference speaker, and an encourager who motivates people to utilize their full potential. She formed the W.I.V.E.S Facebook Group to rally wives to share thoughts, prayers, encouragement and insight. Arts in Christian Theatre is another platform she forged that promotes the creative expressions of the arts and is open to all ages. LetGodLead is her weekly teaching/preaching outreach internet program aired on Global7.tv.

Pastor Robyn Edwards currently serves as the Executive Associate Pastor of Ministry at The International Gathering at Beth Rapha in Pomona, New York, under the leadership of Bishop Jacqueline E. McCullough. She holds a Bachelor of Theology Degree from the Vision International University in Jamaica, NY, and has received her Master's and Doctorate degrees in Biblical Counseling from the Beth Rapha Christian College and Theological Seminary. A prolific biblical counselor by gifting, administrator by trade, and "teacher from God," Pastor Robyn has been qualified and recommended to teach and edify believers with a sensitive yet powerfully insightful approach captured largely in part by her own personal experiences with God.

Donovan & Jennifer Freeman have been married for 34years and have known each other for over 40 years. They met at a Community College as teenagers. Their union produced three beautiful children. Donovan has been working with the railroad company for over 15 years and Jennifer works in the food industry. They presently worship at Bethel Gospel Tabernacle and their ultimate goal and desire is to serve God and walk in the sufficiency of the scripture.

Ana Harris, student of life and warrior for Christ. A wife and mother of two, aspiring entrepreneur. A woman committed to glorify God with her life and testimony because she know our God never fails.

Shanay Y. Howard was born 1/1/86 and is married to Isaac Howard. Together they have four children, three living: Oluwasegun "Duro" Durosinmi, Ciela Joy, Tehila Heaven-Lynn, and one who passed away – their first born Heaven Renée. Shanay has a Master's Degree in Counselor Education and is a licensed school counselor and educational consultant. In addition, Shanay is an ordained minister who loves working in youth and young adult ministry. She presently resides in Sterling, Virginia.

Pauline Hunter is the proud mother of five wonderful adult children and currently lives in Brooklyn with her husband of 36 years. She recently retired with 30 years of service from the New York City Department of Education as a Special Education teacher. Pauline is an avid reader which is evidenced by the library in her home and an insatiable thirst for knowledge. With two Master's Degrees in Education and presently working on a Bachelor's Degree in Ministerial Studies, she still finds time to read. Pauline is also a humanitarian who abhors injustice on any level, but mostly against women, the elderly and children. Pauline loves her family, especially her grandchildren who bring her so much joy.

Elaina Monrae is a mother, wife, humanitarian and first-time author. With a lifetime of deep, unique personal experiences, Elaina hopes to share many more stories with future readers.

 **Raymond Ramos** has a long history of serving his country and NYC as an Army National Guard member, a Deputy Director at the NYC Department of Transportation, and a decorated member for over twenty years of the New York Police Department. His military experience while serving in Bosnia and Iraq inspired him to help others fight through adversity to realize their full potential. Raymond's interactions with the most challenging communities while serving with the NYPD fueled his desire to mentor young men, hence he established Project: H.Y.P.E. (Helping Young People Evolve). Ray resides in New York City with his wife, Princess and is the father of three daughters Janelle, Octavia, Amber, his son Malik, and grandson Onyx.

 **Lisa Angel Ray** is an author, motivational speaker, producer, radio host, MC and recent founder of ANGELS HEARTS FOR HOPE FOUNDATION INC., a non-profit to bring awareness to Multiple Sclerosis. She is an MS Warrior fighting to overcome MS, support, uplift and inspire others to connect to their purpose. She is an avid lover of the arts and writes songs, poetry, skits, short stories and more. Lisa brings her business experience in education, finance, promotions, marketing, customer service, creative writing, love of people and positive energy to all she encounters. She walks by faith and not by sight. Lisa trusts in God and believes according to Jeremiah 29:11 *"For I know the plans I have for you, to prosper and not harm you, plans for hope and a future."*

Made in the USA
Middletown, DE
07 November 2021

51609998R00137